THE PLAYERS

the
players

taking hollywood for a ride

jo reynolds

MAINSTREAM
PUBLISHING

EDINBURGH AND LONDON

First published in Great Britain in 2006 by
MAINSTREAM PUBLISHING COMPANY
(EDINBURGH) LTD
7 Albany Street
Edinburgh EH1 3UG

ISBN 1 84596 060 2

A catalogue record for this book is
available from the British Library

Typeset in ITC New Baskerville and Billboard

Printed and bound in Great Britain by
Cox & Wyman Ltd

FOR BELLA

THE PLAYER

'I know I've had more than my fair share but that don't stop me wanting more – for a start I've had four wives – Mark One's Jewish – we've got two Jewish daughters – Mark Two's Indian from Guyana – we've got two Anglo-Indian daughters – Mark Three's black from the Dominican Republic – we've got no children – Mark Four's English – I mentally adopted her two daughters – I love every one of them – I've lived in England, Trinidad, Spain, Canada, Scotland, Guyana and the United States – I've had bars, clubs and restaurants in London and Marbella – I've had gold mines in Canada – I've been a millionaire – twice – and lost it – twice – but at one stage I had a villa in Spain, an apartment in London and another in New York – life was good

– and it all came from the cab – it goes to show –
you can make a living from the front of a cab –
and a bloody *fortune* from the back . . .'

THE NIGHT OF THE HUNTER

If I kept a diary, I'd have spilt a lot of ink on 1 January 1994. But I don't need a diary to remember the day I met Colin Hayday. Although it was over a decade ago, I won't forget my first impression: frankly, I didn't like him.

It was approaching midnight when I returned to London after spending Christmas with my parents. Paddington Station was particularly foreboding on that frozen winter's night. I was in a defeated mood, waiting impatiently for a taxi in an endless queue. I passed the time jotting pretentious notes in the elegant leather-bound journal I'd been given for Christmas. I've still got that journal and know exactly what I wrote:

Hollow trains lay like coffins in the giant mausoleum that Paddington Station becomes after midnight. The place was shrouded in an atmosphere of cruel abandon that reached all the way to the rafters where dripping wrought iron arches caged restless pigeons, hiding from the sleet.

Boo hoo!

A hundred feet below, all I wanted was to get home as fast as possible because I'd already endured a gruelling eight-hour journey. My train had finally given up ploughing snow at Reading, and I'd been forced to finish my journey in a coach. At six foot six, I'm especially unsuited to coach travel. The legroom would have challenged a contortionist, and I found myself forced to sit in a position that even an advanced yogi would consider impossible.

Few cab drivers can have been working that night as the taxis were rolling in as infrequently as winning lottery balls. I considered using the Underground until I remembered I'd missed the last train. I resigned myself to waiting and prayed I wouldn't get a gabby cabbie.

I didn't notice Colin himself when we converged at the head of our respective queues. I stooped under the hunchbacked roof of his old-style cab without seeing his face. The cab was immaculate but abattoir cold. I tried to turn on the heating but only managed to blast the cabin with more cold air. I abandoned the controls and wrapped myself into the furthest corner of the cabin, still steamed up from the last passenger, and rubbed my bruised knees to encourage the return of the circulation I'd lost on the coach. Ignoring Colin, I cleared a porthole with my sleeve and as we pulled away I noticed an old woman who was left in the queue behind me. I should have noticed her before and been a gentleman and let her go ahead of me, but I hadn't and that made me feel even worse.

I was cocooned in gloom when Colin's booming voice ricocheted round the cabin.

'Where are you taking me? Anywhere interesting?'

That made me feel worse still: I'd got a gabby cabbie. I wished I'd taken the Tube. I wished I'd walked. No, I wished I'd cut my legs off and taken an ambulance.

But his delivery was so relentlessly cheerful I felt obliged to park my sulk. His accent was genuine cockney, and the volume was explained by a speaker and microphone arrangement that Colin had had installed in order to hear his punters over the deafening grandpa's gargle of the cab's diesel engine. These systems are common now, but Colin's was one of the first.

'Ladbroke Grove, please,' I said curtly, hoping to deter further conversation.

'Cheer up. One day it'll be Holland Park.'

I didn't reply because I couldn't bear any more of his pep talk. Within thirty seconds of meeting Colin I'd prejudged him to be a man obsessed with money – and the sound of his own voice.

'What do you do for a living? Anything interesting?' he asked, fixing me via the rear-view mirror. I noticed his glasses had thick lenses, like those of Eldon Tyrell, the genius robot inventor in *Blade Runner*. I really didn't want to join his conversation; he seemed quite capable of conducting the whole thing on his own.

'I write,' I said limply. It was the rehearsed and deliberately vague answer I always used. I never said, 'I'm a screenwriter', because that sounded too purposeful and implied I earned a living from my writing when, in truth, I hadn't been paid for a single word. I knew I was a failure, but I avoided being a liar as well.

'What do you write?' His voice seemed to be getting louder; it felt like an interrogation. I think he'd only just had the PA system installed and had forgotten to stop shouting.

'High concept,' I said, still reluctant to talk to him but pleased enough to show off what little Hollywood-speak I knew.

'What the fuck's that?' It was a fair question and squarely put. High concept is dated terminology now, but in the mid-'90s it was the catch-all phrase for a film based on one big idea. High-concept films can be pitched in one line because the concept is poster simple. *Alien* is a good example. The pitch would be nothing more than '*Jaws* in space'. Another example is *Groundhog Day*: 'a man wakes up to find every day the same'. *Groundhog Day* is stratospherically high concept and demonstrates perfectly the common denominator of all high-concept films: they are never based on reality.

I was about to explain this further to Colin, but he took charge of my favourite subject with a few rapier questions. His brief interrogation reduced my life to nothing – just like this:

'What do you write? Books?'

'Films.'

'Anything made?'

'No.' Worst two letters in the world.

'Well, don't you worry about that. I've got a good story for you.' I couldn't tell whether his tone was gloating or pitying. I decided it was both. He was the worldly-wise traveller throwing scraps at the poor blind boy. I would have been offended, but it was a delicious story and it started like this:

'I know I've had more than my fair share but that don't stop me wanting more – for a start I've had four wives . . .'

I'd started the journey sitting as far from Colin as possible but finished it with my nose a foot from the glass partition. Colin neatly wrapped up his story to coincide with the end of my journey. He braked hard and as the cab scraped its nails to a stop outside my house I nearly toppled onto the floor. I clambered out and was suddenly all smiles, a sharp contrast to the face I'd worn at the start. He opened his passenger window to take my money. It was the first time I saw his face properly. I clocked him as fifty, nearly twice my age back then. He was immaculately groomed and good looking in a cheekbone sort of way. He was only let down by the bottle-thick lenses. The strong frames and accent prompted me to log him as a Michael Caine look-alike in my mental library of brief encounters.

'You should write that down,' I said, sneaking a glance at my change, a sensible precaution given what I'd just heard.

'I can't. I'm dyslexic.'

I was surprised by his candour, but before I could think of a delicate reply he handed me a business card.

'If *you* want to write it, give me a bell.'

I read the card: COLIN HAYDAY – PURVEYOR.

'Purveyor?' I asked. 'Purveyor of what?'

Colin smiled.

'Whatever the fuck you like!'

His owl's eyes flickered like the last candle on a birthday cake.

And then he was gone.

DANGEROUS LIAISONS

I rushed upstairs and hadn't even shut the front door to the flat before I started ranting to my girlfriend about the encounter.

'I've just met this extraordinary cab driver.'

She didn't share my excitement, but she had no reason to: it was well after midnight, she'd been asleep, and I'd re-routed a polar draught into our bedroom.

'Really?' she said.

'He told me an amazing story.'

'Don't tell me. About the people he's had in the back of his cab?' she said, pulling the duvet over her head.

'He's been looking for a writer for years.'

'He'll pay you, right?' she asked from under the covers.

'We didn't talk about that.'

She pulled the duvet down to look at me. She smiled and shook her head in mock exasperation. She'd put up with my struggling-artist routine for years. And I couldn't dismiss her immediate suspicions about Colin's finances because he had just admitted to being bankrupt. But I was more concerned by the other stuff he'd told me: the dangerous stuff, the stuff that could get me killed, the stuff that could get us killed. I didn't share my paranoid imaginings on that particularly starless night. But I did make a point of double-locking our front door.

The next morning I woke alone, as my girlfriend had already left for work. I immediately thought of the post. Spending all day alone makes a visit from the postman a major event. It can set the mood for the whole day. I had sent my latest high-concept script to various London production companies a month before Christmas and figured I was due some responses.

Our flat was the second floor of a converted but not soundproofed Victorian townhouse. Sharing such a building soon exposes the neighbours' routines, often in alarming detail. I'd heard the guy below leave for the City, and everyone above had tap danced down the communal stairs except

Duncan, a feckless 'trustafarian' in the flat directly above who always masturbated till midday – the stretched soundtrack on his favourite Greek porn video was unmistakable. Even though I was wearing only boxer shorts, I braved the cold and cantered downstairs to the communal front door.

Enough letters and bills and junk mail had landed on the welcome mat to form a pile as unappealing as a tramp's pizza. I knew immediately that one of the wholemeal brown envelopes contained my latest script. I'm not claiming to be Hercule Poirot; no deduction was involved. I knew because one of the green plastic spiral binders I'd chosen to make my scripts stand out had torn through the manhandled envelope; even the postman had no regard for my writing. I knew it had been rejected because people don't return what they want. I also knew that 'Unfortunately' would be the first word to appear on line three of the covering letter – because it always was. I knew this because I'd written six scripts and I'd had enough 'unfortunately' letters to wallpaper the Hollywood sign – both sides. I was the most prolific failed screenwriter in London. No: the world.

Upstairs, I ignored the covering letter because knowing exactly which production company was feeling unfortunate wouldn't make my rejection any less bruising. I resolved to bury the subject instantly and dropped the dog-eared package into the bin. I then found myself dwelling on all the doomed symbolism this implied.

I couldn't understand why they hadn't liked the script. High concept couldn't get any higher without actually joining NASA. It was certainly better than some of my previous efforts: the one about the house that had a crush on its owner or the one about the toothless vampire or the one about the invisible celebrity. But then I stopped listing my life's work, as I realised that absolutely nothing I'd ever written bore any relationship to life itself. On that second day of the New Year, I'd woken up to the harsh realisation that I was a complete dreamer. It was time for a major rethink. High concept was letting me down badly. I needed to go low. I needed to get in the gutter. I needed to get real.

Then I remembered Colin. I looked for his business card and plucked it from the bin. I then found myself dwelling on all the hopeful symbolism this implied. Then I saw that word: 'Purveyor'.

'Purveyor, my arse!' I said out loud. It was as ridiculous as talking to yourself. And there was only a mobile number on the card. No address, no landline, no fax, no VAT number, no company registration number. It looked dodgy. But it had been a bloody good story. It had been bloody. And it had been real.

I picked up the phone and soon discovered that because Colin is an opportunist he reacts instantly.

'What are you doing right now?' he said.

While I waited for him to arrive, I took out my Christmas journal and started to make notes about what Colin had told me the night before.

THE SILENCE OF THE LAMBS

Back in his taxi, after Colin had got my attention by telling me about how many wives he'd had and lost, and how many millions he'd had and lost, his pitch moved to how his story began:

'It all started in what I call "Lawyerland" – Lincoln's Inn Fields – where the big lawyers have their offices. Anyway, this lawyer gets in. He was from Burma originally. I won't tell you his name, but let's call him Alex – young guy – maybe thirty. He went to Eton and looks the part – three-piece whistle – until you look close – he's a bit shabby round the edges – kind of guy who only irons his shirt where it shows. Anyway, he's a sad sod – homesick. All he wants is to run home to Mummy in Rangoon. I reckon he was bullied at school, but he was bloody clever and he obviously passed his exams. So I say to him, "What do you do for a living? Anything interesting?" "Lawyer," he says. "You're a lawyer and you're not happy? Some people are never satisfied," I told him.

'So we get to Piccadilly and I decide it's time to cheer him up. Besides, it's always useful to know a lawyer. I pull over outside his hotel, the Ritz. "Are you meeting anyone here?" I say. He says no, so I say, "Let me buy you a drink." He's a bit surprised. "Don't worry, I'm not gay," I tell him.

'He's got nothing else to do, so he orders a double whisky with lots of ice. Eventually, I get him talking. "I want out," he says. "Out of what?" I say. "Everything. London. All of it." "How far would you go?" "What do you mean?" he says. "How far would you go to get what you want?" But he's smart, isn't he? He realises I'm asking him if he'll break the law. He says nothing. So I try again.

'"Would you cross the line?" "*Absolutely not*," he says. I tell him Howard Hughes said every man has his price. "Not me," he says. "If I put a gun to your head, you'll do as I say. That's your price," I tell him. I think that scared him coz he goes all quiet. But then he says, "It would have to be a bloody high price." HOOKED HIM!

'"How high's high?" He laughs and says,

"Forgive me – but a fuck of a lot more than a cab driver can come up with!" "A million?" I say. He says nothing. "*Ten* million?" I say. He finishes his drink in one – he wants to go. "More than ten million?" I say, impressed. "A lot more," he says. GOT HIM!

"'So you would cross the line," I say. He gets up to go. "I said NO," he says, raising his voice, trying to be the little tough guy. "But you thought about it," I said.'

In my journal, I drew a line down the middle of the page to create two columns: one for Colin's GOOD traits and one for the BAD. The first entry on the plus side was: THOUGHTFUL. Colin's attempt to raise Alex's spirits was a Samaritan gesture, even if his generosity masked the first entry in the bad column: SCHEMING. I recalled Colin had asked both Alex and I a lot of cryptic questions; it kept him in control of the conversation. I wrote CONTROL FREAK in the bad column. I also remembered something else both Alex and I had experienced on our first encounters with Colin: he dismisses pessimism in others. I added CHEERFUL to the good column. So far it was two all: evenly matched – half good, half bad. Then I wrote down a concern I could no longer ignore: Colin seemed to be extremely at ease with the idea of breaking the law. I wrote DISHONEST in the bad column. And as he was equally comfortable threatening to be VIOLENT, that went down as well. The bad points were adding up.

GOODFELLAS

Back on my first journey with Colin, I'd asked him how the lawyer had fitted in, but he'd insisted I 'Hang on'. It was his pitch and he was telling it his way. Instead, my raconteur told me about the men he called The Ties.

'I was driving past The Admiral Codrington in South Ken. I'm not good on pubs coz I don't drink, but I remember that one coz it's where I picked up The Ties. One was a toff and one wasn't – both were pissed. I like to keep things simple, so I'll call one The Toff and the other The Eastender. The Toff dressed Oxford Street – really flashy tie. The Eastender was Jermyn Street – neat stripy tie. I remember what they were wearing coz you'd expect it to be the other way round.

'"Cheyne Walk and then Notting Hill," says The Toff without a please. No one likes being treated like a servant, but I keep quiet because they were in the middle of an interesting conversation – they're talking money.

'"I think they'd let it go for fifty million," says The Toff. That got me interested. "Why are they selling?" says The Eastender. "Going out of business," says The Toff. The Eastender's amazed. "*Speyhawk*?" he says. Then The Toff says something about NatWest wanting to buy it but they can't – they were trapped by their lease.

'But before I could get any more, The Toff notices we're home. "STOP!" he shouts, the little Hitler, so I hit the brakes – hard. They roll round in the back, and the next thing I know The Eastender's chucking up in the back – all over my fucking carpet. So I chuck them both out and nick a nifty for the cleaning bill. They'd pissed me off. I was going to have to clean up their mess. I was going to give them a slap, but then I realise they've given me much more than fifty quid.

'Now, I like to keep my ears open because you often hear more than you're meant to. Those boys used the word "lease", so they must've been in the property business. And they knew details about NatWest and Speyhawk, so they must've been on the inside. I'd heard of Speyhawk – they were big in property – and if they're going out of business, it must've been their building they're going to sell cheap. Plus they said NatWest were the tenants. All I had to do was find out the buildings Speyhawk owned and then narrow it down to the one NatWest rented. It'd only be a couple of calls. Then all I had to do was go to Speyhawk and tell them I was interested in buying their building.'

I remembered being impressed by all that. He'd worked out the whole jigsaw puzzle – even if, to the rest of the world, all he had was a few pieces of sky. He hadn't been at all fazed by the mention of such huge sums. But how was a cab driver going to set up a multi-million-pound property deal? Then I remembered he'd cleverly tucked away a big-time lawyer for a rainy day.

Back on my good and bad columns I wrote CUNNING on the good side and doodled a fox in the margin. As it looked more like a husky dog, I abandoned it and added OPPORTUNIST to my list of positives. The columns were equally matched again.

I started a new page for The Ties and entitled it HOT TIP. I made another two columns and topped them with THE TOFF and THE EASTENDER. But because I'm not Colin and don't always 'keep things simple', I started making reams of notes about The Ties, including, for some reason, extensive details about their clothing. I imagined The Toff dressed like a *Miami Vice* pimp – in autumn. I put his suit down as the colour of algae and his loafers as suede, a shade of bindweed. I guessed his tie was Versace at a time when the now murdered couturier liked to combine heraldic symbols with tiger print. I imagined The Eastender dressed like Prince Charles and had him wearing a lot of ampersands: New & Lingwood brogues, a double-breasted Gieves & Hawkes suit, a Turnbull & Asser shirt and a red & blue striped tie.

But I put the brakes on my sartorial tour when I remembered Colin had threatened to 'slap' The Ties. I turned back a page and underlined <u>VIOLENT</u>, nudging his bad traits into the lead again.

ICE COLD IN ALEX

I'd been fascinated by his hot property tip. But I couldn't work out what a cab driver wanted to do with a skyscraper. This is what he told me:

'So I find the building easy – a couple of calls. But if I was going to buy it, I'd need help – serious help – and Alex was all I had. So I go back to Lawyerland. I know I've got the right square, but I don't know which office is his. So I park on the corner near the Tube, every morning from seven – I want to catch him going to work. It's a week before I see him and it's eleven o'clock – I needn't have been the early bird to catch that little worm.

'Anyway, I follow him into his office. It's all very smart – all oak and marble – but I'm in a whistle, so I look the part. Alex is getting a bollocking from his boss for being late. His name's Smedley – it's a slimy name and he's a slimy sod. No wonder Alex wants out. I don't stand for bullies, so I try to help Alex out.

"'Morning, Alex. Am I early for my appointment?" Of course, he's bloody surprised to see me, but he gets the hint and uses me as his excuse to leave. When we get to his office, he says, "How did you find me?" I tell him straight: "I followed you." Alex starts to sweat. I must say he was always pretty damp.

'Anyway, I try the charm and say, "Something special's come up you might like." He still don't want to talk, so I lean on him a bit. "I can always come back tomorrow," I say. He gets the hint.

'Anyway, I take him to the building and I tell him about the tip I heard. And he says, "But why do you want the building?" He hasn't got it. "It's not the building I want, it's the mortgage – the loan – the money." He still hasn't got it. So I spell it out: "We're going to steal it!" He starts to panic. "*We*?" he says. "Why do you need me?" "To make me look kosher," I say. "Look. It's simple." So I explain: I tell him all we have to do is set up a property company and cook the books so it looks like it's been trading for a few years. Then we make an offer on the building and apply for a mortgage. I tell him the tenants already pay handsome rent, so the figures will stack up. And when we get the mortgage, we get the bank to transfer the money to my lawyer's account as standard.

'"That's you," I tell him. "Finally, and here's the simple bit," I say, "you don't transfer the money to Speyhawk, you transfer it to us." He still don't look happy, so I point out, "You get half. That's twenty-five million quid. Now, I'm only a fucking cab driver, but is that enough for you?" At last, he smiles. "Look, Alex," I tell him. "You said you wanted out. You're not going to get another chance like this. But we've got to move fast. This building ain't going to hang around." That always works. Offer something and take it away – people always want it more. Well, it was enough for him. "Let me think about it," he says. GOT HIM.'

It was a great story. But I had been extremely suspicious. 'Why did he come on board so easily?' I'd said from the back seat.

'Don't you worry,' Colin had said. 'You'll find out why later.'

So there it was: that's when he told me he was a con man. I put down another entry on the bad list: CON MAN. That put bad well into the lead.

THE ODD COUPLE

My recollections were interrupted by an excessively long buzz on the door. There was no mistaking an arrival by Mr Colin Hayday.

'Come up. First floor,' I said over the intercom.

'You come down,' he said, and then I heard his footsteps receding. I wasn't sure about his abruptness: I thought it rude. I stalled, suddenly unsure about getting involved with him at all. He was a SCHEMING CONTROL FREAK and a DISHONEST, VIOLENT CON MAN. If this had been an encounter in a Scorsese film, I'd have been the novice priest and Colin the seasoned gangster. I reminded myself I didn't like him. And he was telling me what to do. I wouldn't tell a stranger what to do. We were completely different. We'd never get on. But why was I judging him? He wasn't all bad. I forced myself to remember he was a THOUGHTFUL, CHEERFUL and CUNNING OPPORTUNIST. It would be interesting if nothing else. And I *did* like his story. That was enough. I ran downstairs.

Colin was waiting on the bottom step wearing an expensive camelhair overcoat like Paul Newman's in *The Color of Money*. He shook my hand, suddenly all polite, and walked back to his cab, double-parked by the bus shelter in front of my house.

'I've got something to show you,' he said, opening the door for me.

'What?' I asked.

'You'll see.'

'I don't like surprises,' I said, immediately regretting the cliché and that I hadn't brought a coat.

I climbed into the back, watched jealously by the shivering commuters who were waiting for a bus only a few feet away.

'Where are you taking me? Anywhere interesting?' I said. He ignored that I'd remembered his line and started the cab.

'I get the idea you're not quite convinced. Thought I'd take you on a quick tour.' His charm disarmed me.

'Can you spare the time?' he added for good

measure. Then he explained how the heating controls worked.

We drove east, past King's Cross Station and then up Pentonville Road towards Islington. We'd only just started going up the hill when he turned a hard left into the car park of two office towers marked with the NatWest Bank logo. Colin parked by the front door in a space reserved for the CEO and stepped out as boldly as a visiting US President. I got out and although I was freezing in my shirtsleeves I was more aware of the security cameras trained on us. Colin didn't seem at all fazed and calmly lit a cigarette. He paced around, blowing jets of smoke at the towers. I looked up at them. There wasn't much to them except their size. Colin had become reflective and wasn't offering much. I was freezing; I hugged my arms and tried to break the ice.

'So this was yours?' I sounded more incredulous than I'd meant to.

He dragged half an inch from his cigarette and flicked the butt into the air. I watched the glowing orange trail arc gracefully across the charcoal sky. The butt landed, jumped, skipped and rolled to a stop just shy of the front door.

'Yes,' he said. 'For a day.'

FRANKENSTEIN

As we drove away from the building, he told me about the man who'd given him the idea to turn his story into a film:

'Two years ago, I'm in Wardour Street, trying to remember the one-way system. This wealthy couple gets in. I know they're wealthy coz they ask for the Savoy. They're "petrols" – petrol tanks – Yanks.

'Anyway, I say to them, "What do you do for a living? Anything interesting?" And she says, all proud, "My husband's in movies." "Any money in it?" I say. "There can be," the man says. Now I like the sound of that, but he don't want to talk, so I turn to her. And she says, "There's money in it if your audience likes your story." "I've got a story for you," I say and off I go.

'When I'm done, the wife looks shocked. "You poor man," she says. "You're right," I said, "I'm skint. That's why I'm back in the cab." I tell them I didn't always drive a cab, but I kept the licence just in case – had it nearly thirty years – was the first exam I passed – was the only exam I passed. Learning every street in London is quite a trick if you can't read. Then the man asks me: "Is it true?" "Yes," I say. "Every last word of it." "It would make a great film," he says. "Go on, then," I say. "No one's stopping you." That surprised him. He wasn't used to being told what to do.

'Anyway, we get to the Savoy and he says, "I'll take a look at the script." "What script?" I say. He's amazed. "You haven't got a script? *Everyone* in Hollywood has a script." "I'm a dyslexic cab driver," I say. "Give me a break." Then he says, "Get a script and I'll take a look. It's a good story." "And you just paid a fiver to hear it," I say. Then I say to him, "What's your name?" But he won't answer. So his wife chips in, "You really don't know anything about the movie business, do you?" "No," I say. "But if there's money in it, I'm willing to learn." And then he gives me a good piece of advice. "One thing you'll learn about Hollywood, it's five per cent inspiration and ninety-five per cent sheer bloody-minded persistence." "So, what *is* your name?" I try again.

His wife's about to answer, but he keeps her quiet and says, "If you're any good, you'll find me."'

'Now,' Colin said to me, '*that* is what I call a challenge.'

CASINO

My tour of Colin's story moved on to Lincoln's Inn Fields, where he showed me Alex's office, and then to South Kensington, where he pointed out the pub where he'd picked up The Ties. By the time we got to my house, the cab's meter had run up seventy-two pounds. He hadn't planned to charge me; he had to keep the meter running for insurance reasons. As I was getting out, Colin shouted through the passenger window, 'Here's the deal. You write it and I'll sell it. We go halves. Fifty-fifty – straight down the line.'

I was impressed a Hollywood hotshot had liked his story. Indeed, having seen for myself where it happened, I liked the story even more. But I wasn't totally convinced.

'I'm sorry to say,' I said, 'but I still can't believe your scam is – well – true.'

That offended him.

'But I've shown you where it happened.'

'With respect, you've shown me some buildings. You could have taken me to any old pub, any old office . . .'

'And spun the whole story round one NatWest sign?'

'Well, you are a con man.' I laughed, hoping it would lift his angry mood. But Colin didn't laugh.

'Don't flatter yourself. Do you think I'd go to all the trouble of inventing something that complicated just for you?' His argument did make sense: his story had been particularly detailed.

'All right, I believe your story. But can I think about it?' It seemed a sensible suggestion.

'No,' he said.

I didn't understand his impatience. We were all but complete strangers and were talking about becoming long-term business partners.

'I've been looking for a writer for two years. I want an answer now.'

I imagined Colin would be good at poker. I'm not. I don't even know the rules.

'Colin, this is a huge undertaking for me. I'm afraid I really am going to have to think about it a little longer.'

'What's to think about?'

I didn't want to answer because my major concern was that I didn't want him as a partner. I figured my whole family, indeed everyone I'd ever met, would think I was insane getting involved with a thieving con man. I tried to relax and expressed my concern as calmly as I could:

'Have the – err – well – police – ever – you know – been – um – involved?'

Colin laughed. 'You're as twitchy as he was.'

'Who?'

'You leave the police to me,' he said, his evasion offering me no comfort.

'Can you write it down or not?' Colin was being more than a little patronising.

'It's not quite that simple, Colin. I'm not a human Dictaphone. Screenwriting is a little more complicated than being some kind of visual stenographer.' I hoped tripping him up with technology might buy me some time.

It didn't. He started up the cab.

'Fine. I'll find someone else.'

And he was gone.

FOR WHOM THE BELL TOLLS

It was the first time a good story, a real story, a
true story, had landed at my feet, and I'd kicked it
away. But if Colin was behaving like that at the
honeymoon stage of the relationship, we'd be
divorced in a week. He'd be the seven-day itch
you couldn't scratch. But I wouldn't have to work
with him in person, day in, day out. He was
dyslexic. Once I'd finished my research, there was
no reason for him to interfere at all.

But if I was doing all the writing, why should he
get half? After all, if I wrote a script about anyone
else, I wouldn't have to give them anything. But
then again, it was his story and he was going to do
all the selling – something I had no confidence
about doing myself, given my failed past
attempts. And it was a damn good story. If I didn't

write it, he'd find someone else. Probably the someone else who was getting into his cab right at that moment.

I couldn't decide. I rang my father. The call made me nervous because he's extremely clever. Scholarship clever. Oxford clever. Intimidating clever. And he's successful; he worked in the City. But above all, he's extremely honourable. I was nervous because I desperately wanted him to approve of my new venture, yet I knew he would never do business with Colin. Consequently, I didn't admit Colin was a con man.

'I don't know him, but he's got a very good story,' I said and then tried to pitch it. I wasn't impressive.

'Do you trust him?' he said cleverly, seeing the point immediately.

'Absolutely,' I said, too ashamed to admit I was even contemplating doing business with a thief.

'If he's bringing something to the partnership that you value, don't deny him his fair share,' he said honourably.

'Of course,' I said, pretending I'd known the answer all along. Then I realised I didn't know what he meant.

'So what is fair?' I hoped having a second go didn't make me sound too thick.

'If his story's as good as you say, you're not in a position to be greedy,' he said. He must have thought I was thick and greedy.

'Good advice, Pa,' I said, hoping flattery would distract him. If I was being thick and greedy, I might at least be charming about it.

'But if you go ahead, get a contract drawn up between you.'

'Yes, you're right,' I agreed instantly.

Now I was thick, greedy, charmless – and a sycophant.

My father had raised all the important points, but still I couldn't decide. I phoned my mother for a second opinion. Whereas my father, the honourable businessman, was the ultimate font of measured yet always gentlemanly advice, my mother, the artist, was excited by anything new and laughed at the risks. 'Go for it, darling,' she said grandly.

As I felt guilty about having withheld Colin's criminal past from my father, I was more forthcoming with my mother.

'I think he's a bit dodgy, Ma,' I said.

'It all sounds very thrilling to me,' she said. 'You were clearly meant to meet him.'

I was expecting that advice. My mother was a big fan of what was 'meant to be' and read her horoscope daily in the hope of discovering what new excitements fate had in store.

So I took my parents' advice and resolved to go fifty-fifty to secure the story that might change my career. Well, start my career. Fifty-fifty made sense. Colin's story was great. If anything, I was the liability in the partnership. I was the untested one. He was doing me a favour. There and then, I decided I'd do it. Good decision. I was good at this. Maybe I'd take up poker.

I had no idea what fifty-fifty would mean in raw-fingered cash because, as I didn't need to remind myself, I'd never sold a script before. I didn't know what the going rate was. I presumed a script for a massive blockbuster would sell for more than one for some tiny arthouse creation, but I wasn't sure whether there was a formula. I'd once read in a film magazine about a writer being paid two per cent of the budget, but that wouldn't equate to much unless Tom Cruise was saying the words.

But just to make triply sure I was doing the right thing, I rang my girlfriend, who was still at work. She always worked late. She said, 'Don't do it.'

'My mother said I should,' I pointed out.

'Did you tell her he's a violent criminal?'

'Well, not exactly.'

'Well, if you had, I'm sure she'd have said the same. Look, darling, he's a con man. He said so himself. He'll rip you off.'

She was right. Of course she was right. She was always right. I couldn't work with a criminal. I could never trust him.

I phoned Colin. I'd toyed with the idea of simply ignoring him. He had just stormed off. But I decided I'd be polite. The least I could do was say no in person.

EYES WIDE SHUT

'Have you changed your mind?' was the first thing Colin said to me over the phone.

'No. I'm afraid not.'

'Why are you calling me, then?'

'I've been thinking about it and I'm not sure . . .'

'What about?'

I didn't know how to phrase it without offending him again.

'You don't trust me, do you?' His direct challenge caught me off guard.

'Well, I must say, my girlfriend thinks you might rip me off,' I said, immediately feeling like a coward for hiding behind her.

'Are you calling me a thief?' he said, raising his voice.

'I'm sorry – but – I seem to be, yes.'

Things had suddenly become distinctly chilly between us; it was not encouraging, as our relationship was already only one degree from frostbite.

'I'm coming round,' he said.

That made me even more nervous: he'd sounded threatening.

WHERE ANGELS FEAR TO TREAD

An hour later, still fearing his raging mood, I'd reluctantly agreed to let Colin drive me to Soho.

'I'm going to prove to you,' he'd said, 'that I look after my business partners.'

It was dark by the time he parked outside what is now the Red Fort Restaurant in Dean Street. It's opposite Quo Vadis, now also a restaurant, but in the 1860s, Colin told me, it was where Karl Marx wrote part of his anti-capitalist treatise *Das Kapital*.

'Twenty years ago, I pull up in this exact spot and where you're sitting now is a guy who owns that club. His name's Ignatius and it ain't the Red Fort back then, it's a hostess club called Dominique's.

'Well, we get talking business and he says, "Do you want to come in?" So he shows me round and I'm telling you, it's as empty as a grave. "What do you think of my club?" he says. "What club?" I say. "It's empty. It's a bloody warehouse." He don't like that, so I say, "But I can fill it for you. In fact, I'll make you a deal. If I don't fill this place by next weekend, you'll never see me again." "What the hell are you talking about?" he says. "If I fill it, I want half," I say. "Do you think I was born yesterday?" he says. "Not with that grey hair," I tell him. He ain't happy with that either. "Look," I say. "You're going out of business. What difference? I can help you, but if you want a hundred per cent of nothing, then good luck to you." So I head for the door and he calls out, "How will you do it?" "Do we have a deal?" I say, offering my hand. He shook it. "Leave the how to me," I said.'

FAR FROM THE
MADDING CROWD

Colin knew I was desperate to learn how he filled the club, but he made me ask. It was another of his tricks; it kept him in control of the conversation.

'So how did you do it?' I said inevitably.

'There are over twenty-five thousand cabbies in London. Every day, every last one of them has to stop for food and water. Did you know, some old law still lets us take a leak in any street so long as we're hidden by the offside back wheel? Cabbies are the only drivers who can legally take the piss!

'Anyway, we take a break in cab shelters. You seen them? Large wooden sheds on the side of the road – usually green – with a line of cabs outside. Shelters are like private clubs – only taxi drivers are allowed. You can get a full meal there or just a cuppa. You end up in a different shelter every day coz you don't know where your journey will take you. It's like an extended family – only better for gossip. I was going to use the shelters to help Ignatius.

'As soon as I leave Dominique's, I visit every shelter in central London and offer every driver I see this deal: "Any bloke gets in your cab looking for a good time, take him to Dominique's on Dean. Ask for Ignatius on the door and you'll get a fiver. Pass it on." Within four days, Dominique's was full of punters – mostly foreign businessmen, of course, but they know how to spend. Ignatius couldn't believe it. Within a month, he was talking about opening another club. We both made our first million. So that's how I looked after Ignatius.

'All the clubs use my system now. But the finder's fee's gone up. You'll get fifty quid a punter now, so you can imagine what a racket hostess clubs have become.'

I was amazed. He'd made it so simple. Colin's world was so very different to mine, and he was inviting me to become a part of it. Surrounded by Soho's usual nocturnal street scene of neon and flesh, I couldn't help thinking that Karl Marx would be spinning in his grave as fast as a stripper's nipple tassel if he knew the capitalist depravity his neighbours were getting up to.

DAY OF THE JACKAL

On the way home from Soho, I knew it was decision time. There was no doubting Colin's ingenuity, and I really could imagine him being an electrifying salesman. His finder's fee system was convincing, and it was certainly plausible that a fortune could be made in the hostess club business. It was bound to have been shamelessly sleazy, but at least it was legal – mostly. More importantly, he had looked after his partner.

But when I considered exactly what he'd shown me, I worried again that his hostess club evidence might have been invented. He'd only parked me outside yet another building and told me it had made him rich. He hadn't introduced me to anyone who could confirm his claims.

'Do you still see Ignatius?' I asked, hoping to extend a line of enquiry.

'No. He's in Israel, enjoying all the money I made him.'

When we reached my house, he pulled over and took out his wallet. He selected a Polaroid photograph and, as if he'd been reading my mind, passed it through the glass partition. It showed an Indian woman sitting by a swimming pool in front of a huge villa. All the colours had faded to a shade of pale amber, but the photo looked genuine.

'That was my villa in Spain,' he said proudly, sounding like a train robber.

'How did you lose it?' I said.

'I put everything from the clubs into property. I borrowed big time and lost the lot when interest rates tripled in '87.'

I remembered a lot of homeowners being hit badly back then. His explanation made sense, but it didn't raise my confidence in him.

'Look, I've done it before. I can do it again. I promise you, I'll make you rich,' he said.

Perhaps oddly, that didn't impress me either. 'It's not about the money,' I said, returning his photo.

'What is it about, then?'

'It's a good story that I need.'

'And so does every writer.' He meant that as a threat.

'I know you're saying you'll just go and find another writer, but not every writer will want a partner who's a – a dangerous criminal.'

'Well, I was honest enough to tell you. Anyway, I'm not dangerous. I may have – borrowed – stuff, but I don't hit people. And why would I hurt you? I need to keep you sweet.'

Colin was clearly growing impatient. 'Come on. What's your answer?'

I was surprised by his aggressive tone. He certainly wasn't trying to charm me into saying yes. I knew it was my last chance. I'd rejected his previous offer, and he wouldn't ask again.

The significance of the opportunity before me, coupled with my doubts about the man himself, made me extremely nervous and confused. This double shot of anxiety spun the last twenty-four hours into a sort of dying man's slideshow. Everything I feared about him and all my Hollywood dreams became a frenzied montage of laughter and loathing. The carousel soon spun out of control and became a blur of white light that blinded me to everything but the raw facts: I was a failure. He had a great story. I didn't like him. He was a great salesman. He might kill me.

'I'll do it,' I said. My final position was that I didn't trust him, but I was prepared to live with that to get his story. It suddenly felt like I'd pawned my soul.

'I knew you would,' he said. That was annoying. 'When can you start?'

I thought about consulting a diary to pretend I had a life but decided instead to look keen.

'Now.'

'Good,' he said. 'I'll be back in a week. See how you're getting on.'

I climbed from the taxi and stood by the front passenger window. He leant over and thrust his hand at me.

'Fifty-fifty. Let's shake on it,' he said, smiling.

I didn't shake because I remembered what my father had suggested. 'Oh, should we draw up a contract?'

'Your word's good enough for me,' he said, reaching out his hand even further. It was extremely awkward. His word most definitely was not good enough for me, but I didn't want to insult him again by spelling out that I really didn't trust him at all. What would my father have done? I had to be the gentleman. I shook his hand. We were partners.

But as soon as he'd gone, it suddenly didn't seem such a smart deal after all. I was going to do all the work, writing the kind of script I'd never attempted before. And then I'd have to rely on a cab driver I didn't trust to sell it to a film industry he knew absolutely nothing about.

It was the blind leading the blind. It was Mr Magoo giving Mr Stevie Wonder a driving lesson – at night – in the snow – in a minefield.

ROOM AT THE TOP

A writer's fear of the virgin – the blank sheet – is well known. This fear is somewhat calmed in the computer age because the word processor presents a page that can be sullied and then cleaned with the urgent press of just one key. The thought of hammering out page after page on a rusty Remington is all very Ernest Hemingway – but imagine the noise.

I shouldn't overstate the merits of the computer, however, because it was a computer that nearly forced me to give up screenwriting before I'd really begun. A wealthy friend had lent me a laptop for two weeks. This was in the '80s, when a laptop was as expensive as a palace. He'd only lent it to me because he was going scuba diving in Antigua and couldn't guard it himself while underwater.

I had fourteen days to transpose the impermanence of my pencil-filled notebooks into the format of a screenplay. I worked day and night on my first ever script – high concept, of course, this one being the comedy about the toothless vampire – until day eight, when I finally retired (appropriately) just before sunrise, blind with exhaustion.

Some unknown operating system programmer in Silicon Valley, probably enjoying a pizza and a pay rise with Bill Gates right now, had decided in his geek's wisdom that I couldn't avoid the sun until I'd answered a series of simple questions. Did I want to save? Yes or no? Was I sure I wanted to save? Yes or no? Did I want to save and quit? Yes or no? Did I want to rename the file? Yes or no? Did I want to sleep or shut down? Yes or no?

I got one of the questions wrong. Geek 1: Screenwriter Gimp 0. I'd saved the file name but not the file. The virgin was back. Blank screen. Every word of my first script was gone. It was an omen. I couldn't sleep. I was too tired to cry. And, no, I didn't have a back-up. All I had were my pencilled notebooks. Even they were just one rub from nothing.

When I sat down to write Colin's story, I had my own computer. It was a Mac Classic. I loved my

Mac. It didn't frighten me. It didn't ask stupid questions. It didn't do the illogical geek things that PCs do: if I wanted to stop, it didn't make me go to the bloody start menu.

My new script lost its virginity when I typed FADE IN at the top of the first page, on the left, leaving a one-and-a-half-inch margin. Typing FADE IN is a reassuring moment. You're out of the blocks and so far have done nothing wrong. Every screenwriter types FADE IN at the top of the first page, on the left, leaving a one-and-a-half-inch margin. So far, my script was flawless. It was as good as if Robert Towne or William Goldman had been writing it. Between them, those two legendary screenwriters have lent their Midas touch-typing skills to *Chinatown*, *All the President's Men*, *Butch Cassidy and the Sundance Kid*, *Bonnie and Clyde* and *Marathon Man*. Everybody likes at least one of those. It's telling that so few people know the screenwriters' names.

So what was I going to fade in on? A taxi, of course. No. Too obvious. But don't be pretentious. It was about a taxi driver. Why not just get the engine running? Rip right out of the pits. There was no need to be dainty. It wasn't some costume drama requiring a gentle introduction. I didn't need the delicate bob of parasols or the mysterious crunch of gravel on some poplar-lined avenue. Decision. As it was about a taxi driver, I'd start with the taxi. And as he was a man possessed, I'd make it a bit weird, a bit mad. I'd start it at night, in Soho, with lots of neon. I'd make it edgy, jazz-funk shadowy. No, that really was pretentious. Damn. And starting with the cab really was obvious. And boring. It'd be better to start with a tease. That was it. Decision. I'd introduce it as a mysterious thriller – a dangerous thriller. I liked that. My fingers flew into action, hunt'n'peck style.

I faded in on an empty Dutch country road at night. There were windmills and canals. That was a visual cliché, but everyone would know instantly it was Holland. A young Colin, as fearless as a cobra in a crèche, and without the glasses of course, was behind the wheel of a Merc. Next to him was twitchy Alex. I'm afraid I took the obvious route and turned Alex into Hugh Grant. (This decision wasn't meant to be racist; I couldn't think of any Burmese actors who might play the real Alex.)

Cut to some headlights. Two cars, Colin's Merc and a silver Jag, were racing towards each other, about to crash head-on. Colin was screaming at Alex, 'Who are they?' Inevitably, Colin sounded very Michael Caine. I was imagining an angry Alfie. Hugh was terrified. It was serious stuff from

Hugh this time. He wasn't flopping his fringe, but he was stuttering. 'Who the fuck are they?' screamed Colin. Cut. Big mystery. Great.

No. I didn't like it. I deleted the lot. Now what? The screen was blank and so was my mind. The answer was coffee.

While the kettle boiled in our tiny galley kitchen, I did ten dips on the arm of the overstuffed sofa in the sitting room. I must admit that every 'rep' was a struggle. I'm no fitness freak; I'm skinny and long ago gave up the idea of beating Arnold Schwarzenegger in an arm wrestle – or Minnie Mouse for that matter. But if you're going to be skinny, you don't want to be soft skinny. Hard skinny is fine. Soft skinny is awful. I did the dips because I wanted to be honed like a whippet.

I took my coffee back to the study. I surveyed the room. It was a second bedroom that I'd turned into my Hollywood shrine. It was full of all the film paraphernalia I'd collected over the years: an alphabet of film biographies, every how-to-write-a-screenplay book ever written by every screenwriter who'd never sold a script, yards of files containing acres of 'unfortunately' letters, a jammed Super 8 film camera, an angrily dented 16mm Bolex I'd found abandoned in a dustbin in Pimlico and some film stock I kept in a dark corner because my girlfriend wouldn't let me keep it in the fridge.

The room was north-facing, the perfect shadow-free orientation for an artist, but the lack of direct sunlight made it gloomy – that, and the way I'd decorated it. For some reason, I'd ignored the basics of colour theory. I decided to paint the room dark red and then lacquer it with a thick antique varnish. Varnished paint effects were fashionable back then. They recreated the National Trust look I thought was so smart. But sod fashion. I was in an abattoir. The room was almost bleeding. I knew I was writing something real for the first time, but I couldn't write in that oppressive atmosphere. It was time to redecorate.

A week later, the room was brilliant white, so white that sunglasses would have been wise. I liked it, right up to the point when it reminded me of an empty page. Then I remembered it was a week later and I still hadn't faded in on anything. I got down to work. As I prepared to type, I noticed my framed *Blade Runner* poster was crooked. I got up to straighten it. Then I straightened a book. And then I did the whole shelf. Then I regrouped the books by height. Then colour. Then I picked my fingernails. Then I pushed back the cuticles – on my toes. I was about to pedicure my right foot when the door buzzer went.

'Hello?' I said in the unwelcoming tone of someone expecting a Jehovah's Witness.

'It's me,' Colin said.

I panicked. I didn't know what to do. If he found out I'd done nothing, he'd find another writer.

'Am I coming up or what?' he asked, suspicious of my evasion.

'Of course,' I said too eagerly, clearly over-compensating.

Within seconds, Colin was up the stairs and knocking on my front door. I let him in. We shook hands. He always shook my hand. I don't know whether he did this with everyone or just me. It was the first time Colin had been inside the flat, and he scrutinised my home quite blatantly, as if I'd invited him to buy the place. He wiped a dust-hunting digit over the antique furniture, tested the sofa and ended the inspection by picking up a silver-framed photo of my mother from the mantelpiece.

'Who's this?'

'My mother.'

'Good-looking woman,' he said. That wasn't something I wanted to hear from Colin, knowing his track record.

'Don't even think about it, Colin.'

I remember feeling he was being intrusive, but I shouldn't have expected Colin to be subtle.

Then he sniffed the air and said, 'Is that paint?' He'd sussed me. I'd forgotten how overpowering the smell is. Again, I said nothing and tried to distract him by going to the kitchen.

'This is a nice surprise,' I said, stalling.

'I said I'd be back in a week.'

I nodded. Then he noticed my bare right foot.

'Helps me concentrate,' I said, knowing my explanation wouldn't wash.

Colin looked perplexed.

'How's it going?' he said.

'I'm very well, thank you. And you?' Good deflection, I thought. I was good.

'I meant the script.' Ah, he was better.

There was an awkward silence.

'How much have you done?' He was painfully direct.

'Oh, I've made an excellent start on act one.' I hoped this would be enough jargon to confuse him. I flicked on the kettle.

'Coffee?' I asked.

'Never said no to a cup of tea in my life,' he said.

'Sugar?'

'Two, please. Stirred once to the left.' Annoying.

'Brown or white?'

He stared at me, suspicious of the unnecessary detail.

'You haven't started, have you?'

I suppose it didn't take much to expose the truth, but I fought on valiantly to deny it.

'Yes, I have.'

'Show me.'

At last I had to concede defeat.

'Um – I wonder – can I have another week, please?'

TOUCHING THE VOID

A week later, I handed Colin the first five pages. He said nothing. But he weighed them in his hand, and his face mocked my modest output. I tried to justify myself.

'The first five minutes are very important.'

'So's the bloody end,' Colin said, trumping me. 'It's taken you two weeks to do five minutes?' He wasn't letting me off. 'At this rate, we'll still be on it next year.'

I wasn't going to take that. I had to fight back.

'What do you mean "we"? I'm the one doing it. You can do it yourself if you like,' I said, immediately ashamed of the low shot.

'You know I can't,' he said, deliberately making me feel worse.

'Do you want me to read it to you?' I said, trying to deflect a row and be helpful.

'No.'

He sat down on the sofa and moved the first page within range of the reading part of his spectacles. His dyslexia made his reading painfully slow. I could see his lips moving. He sneaked a look over his glasses and caught me staring. I looked away, pretending I hadn't been. I left him to it and went to my bright white study.

It took Colin so long to read those first pages I'd almost forgotten he was still in the flat. He startled me when he poked his head round the study door.

'Yes,' was all he said.

'Well?' I wanted more than one word.

'I like it.' He started to fold the pages, then stopped. 'Can I keep this?'

'Of course.'

'So you liked it?' I said eagerly. A writer seeks feedback like a moth seeks a flame; of course you want praise, but in the absence of that you'll take criticism. Not silence, though. He nodded once.

'Is that it?' I said.

He put the folded pages into his pocket.

'I'll see you in a week.' And he showed himself out.

I was frustrated by the complete lack of feedback until I remembered he was only doing what I'd hoped for in the first place: he wasn't interfering at all.

DIAMONDS ARE FOREVER

Stealing the mortgage money involved turning the loan into something portable, for the simple reason that if you steal fifty million pounds, people will come after you.

'Why not cash?' I said, taking out my journal the next time Colin came round.

'Have you seen fifty million in cash? You couldn't carry it. It's only ever a suitcase in the movies, but you'd never carry fifty million.'

I started making notes and wondered whether Colin thought this made me appear like a cop taking down a statement. But he wasn't deterred.

'You couldn't use sterling because the highest value note in pounds is a hundred and they're bloody rare them red Scottish hundreds. You'd need dollars because they do a thousand-dollar bill, but they're even rarer – the drug dealers have all of them.' I was loving this.

'Say a wad holds a hundred notes, that's one hundred thousand dollars a wad, so ten wads for a million. You might get fifty wads in a suitcase, so you'd need ten suitcases.'

I was imagining the abacus clicking in his head.

'No,' he corrected himself. 'That's in dollars. You'd need eighteen cases for fifty million sterling. And how are two guys going to carry eighteen cases? Nine each? We'd have had to do the job with a bloody octopus! No, two.'

'What about fine art?' I said, hoping I sounded cultured.

'We'd have got done ourselves. Go through all that for a snide Picasso? You must be bloody joking. Mind you, Picasso always paid with a cheque. He knew people would never cash it coz they wanted his autograph.' Colin laughed.

'What about drugs?'

'We didn't want to die.' Colin was treating me like the idiot apprentice. 'You deal at the fifty-million level and you're dealing with people who'll kill you before breakfast.'

'Gold?'

'Too heavy.'

'What else is there?' I felt like the idiot apprentice.

'Diamonds.'

I'm glad I took notes, because they helped me write the next scene: about the diamonds.

Considering it's London's diamond district, Hatton Garden doesn't exactly sparkle. It's just a terraced street of understated shops, all with the word 'Diamond' in the sign above their front doors. I suppose it's modest because diamonds don't have to shout.

Colin was admiring a display in one particular shop window when he noticed a woman inside doing business with an old boy behind the counter. She was clearly in the diamond trade. It wasn't that she was dressed rich, which she was; she had her own eyepiece. Colin said she was 'fifty, fat and feisty'. She reminded him of Ruby Wax – only she had 'more hair and less sex appeal'.

Colin checked the number on the shop – it was fifty-two – and waited until she looked like she was leaving. Then he hit the doorbell. You don't just walk into these shops. The old boy peered through the reinforced-glass front door, checking Colin over before buzzing him in. Colin stayed in the doorway.

'Hello, guv. I'm parked outside,' Colin said casually and then made to leave.

'What do you mean?' the old boy said, instantly suspicious.

'Taxi,' Colin said, smiling to placate him.

'I didn't order one.'

'Number fifty-two?' The old boy shook his head. Colin turned to the woman and smiled. She looked Colin up and down blatantly and then turned her attention to the old boy, who waved Colin away.

Colin ambled to his cab, parked a few yards away. A cigarette later, he noticed the woman leave the shop and start walking down the street. We'll call her Margot Di Varga. She was American, but in the script, to overcome never having met Margot, I imagined her as Helen Mirren. Not because I've met Ms Mirren or that she's anything like Ruby Wax, but because I wanted Margot to be more the solo operator and less the show-off.

'Do you need a ride?' Colin called across the street. Margot turned round and recognised Colin.

'You don't give up,' she said.

'Where we going?' Colin drew his most winning smile. 'It's already paid for if you want it.'

Everyone likes a bargain; she walked over and he opened the door.

'The Savoy, please.' The word 'Savoy' made Colin hold his smile. Not only because it confirmed he was dealing with someone of means but also because people who stay in hotels generally don't live locally. As his escape plan relied on him leaving the country, his new passenger became his new target.

Colin sparked up the cab and was about to head to the main road at the end of Hatton Garden when he noticed the heavy traffic.

'Don't worry,' Colin said. 'I know a short cut.'

He reversed twenty yards and then accelerated down a side road dotted with a speed-calming bump every thirty yards or so. The taxi squealed to mount the first hurdle. They rode the bump in tandem, like a slomo pair of rodeo riders. The movement was overtly sexual. They ignored each other. They rode the next bump a little harder. Colin looked at Margot via the rear-view mirror to apologise, but she ignored him. They rode the third bump more cautiously. Still, she ignored him. The fourth was so slow she couldn't help looking to see what he was up to. But that time he ignored her. They took the last bump hard. Their eyes met. She broke away first. When she looked back, he was still staring.

The diamond connection had been made.

LADY CHATTERLEY'S LOVER

Colin drove Margot anti-clockwise round the Savoy's front turning circle. This is the only road in England that permits driving on the right. Colin tells me this arrangement ensures Savoy customers can avoid the rain, as they are always delivered to the hotel under the protection of the front door's grand canopy.

Colin slowed to a smooth halt and Margot got out. He was about to speak to her, but she sauntered off. He'd offered her a free ride and she'd taken it. She hadn't even thanked him. Maybe she meant him to follow her in. He parked up at the back of the taxi rank, slipped the doorman a fiver to guard his cab and spun the revolving door.

Five minutes later, he was standing outside the

door to her hotel room. Was he going to make a
fool of himself? He had to find out: he needed
those diamonds. He took a breath and knocked.
Margot answered immediately. She didn't look
surprised to see him; she'd been waiting. She
stepped back into the room to let him in. Neither
of them spoke.

They stayed silent throughout the shag – that's
the word Colin used to describe it. He said you
definitely wouldn't call it making love. Although
in reality they were the same age, to keep their
encounter unusual in the script, I staged a toy-boy
scenario with a thirty-year-old Colin opposite
Margot as the older woman.

When they'd both sighed, Margot was the first
to speak.

'What's your name?'

Colin was quick to realise he'd need an alter ego.

'Roy. You?' Colin was using his middle name.

'Margot. Now we know each other, you can tell
me the truth. Was that just a mercy fuck?' Margot
was always direct.

'What do you mean?'

'Were you just doing an old gal a favour?'

'You're the one doing favours. I'm just a cab
driver. You're the class.'

She smiled at the compliment.

Colin was in the en-suite bathroom tidying up; apparently Margot supplied the prophylactic. He'd left her on the bed next door. Now was the time to make his move. He called from the bathroom, 'You've done me a favour. I'd like to put some business your way.'

Margot appeared in the doorway. 'What kind of business?'

'You're obviously in diamonds. I know a guy who might be interested in getting hold of one or two,' he said casually.

'I don't do engagement rings.' Margot wasn't the marrying kind; she wore a lot of expensive rings, but none on her wedding finger.

'Can you do fifty million quid's worth?' he said.

Margot arched a heavily plucked eyebrow.

'You know some wealthy people.'

'My dad always said, if you want to be rich, mix with the rich.'

'Is he rich?'

Colin laughed away the subject.

'Where are you based?' he said.

'Amsterdam.'

'That's perfect. My guy's in Europe all the time.'

'What's your guy's name?' She was humouring him, bemused that a cab driver was playing the cocky businessman.

Colin hesitated before answering. 'Alexander Warwick. He's a lawyer.'

'Probably represents someone,' she said.

'Probably.'

'How do you know him?'

'Met him in the cab.'

'You know a lot about him.'

'I like to learn a lot about my passengers.' Colin smiled.

'I don't like to mix business with pleasure,' she said, suddenly taking charge. 'But I'll meet him. If I like him, then maybe. But it's only a maybe, and only if I like him.'

And then she took Colin back to the rodeo.

LEAVING LAS VEGAS

When Colin phoned Alex to report he'd found a diamond broker, Alex was unusually elated and decided to extend the high by celebrating. Because he was shy, he chose to celebrate alone. And because he was one of life's secret gamblers, roulette was how he wanted to spin his way beyond the stratosphere. He wanted even more good news because that's what gamblers are like: one orgasm is never enough.

Insomnia had led him to gambling. He'd tried to end a run of sleepless nights, fretting over homesickness, by distracting himself with long walks in the small hours. Boredom, curiosity and a particularly long walk across three postcodes had delivered him to his first roulette wheel at the Ritz Casino. At that time of night, there was nothing else to do. Gambling was one of the few nocturnal hobbies London allowed. Back in the early '90s it was the only capital city in the world that shut at midnight.

London casinos are not glamorous places. They're full of mostly sad, mostly single men, mostly dreaming that Lady Luck will move closer to their baize. Every flush of success is a flash of stockinged thigh to them, but real victory is as elusive as a hooker's kiss. Gambling is the kind of sex that has to be paid for but doesn't even give a receipt. Alex didn't mind; his loneliness excused his fumbling because he'd finally found somewhere dark to hide. Since his very first date, he was a hopelessly clumsy lover: he learnt nothing and lost heavily. He continued because he felt safe with Lady Luck – and one day she might even say yes.

When Alex hailed a cab outside his office, he didn't tell anyone he was going out for another whirlwind romance: especially not Colin. He also didn't tell the people he owed money to, the same people who'd paid for all his dates. But he didn't have to, because they already knew. They were following him: in a silver Jag.

OF MICE AND MEN

The next day, Colin wanted to check with Alex on the progress of their fake property company. The mechanics of setting one up are straightforward and the first stage was entirely legal. Alex was going to buy a dormant company 'off the shelf' from Companies House, the national body based in London that administrates British companies. Buying a company off the shelf is a common way of starting a new business because it's cheap – around a hundred pounds; it's a bargain because the administration involved in establishing the company has already been done. Put simply, off-the-shelf companies have ceased trading but have yet to be unregistered. Crucially, this gives them a start date that isn't yesterday, exactly what a con man needs if he wants to look established or, Colin's word, kosher.

The second stage – the crooked stage – was to bridge the gap between the registration date and the present one. To do this, false trading figures would be invented to make the company look as if it had been trading profitably for a respectable amount of time. That was the plan. This was the detail:

Colin parked up outside Alex's office and called him from his mobile, one of those early-style bricks. Alex didn't sound too chirpy. It was nothing to do with fledgling mobile technology. The night before, Alex's debt collectors had accosted him – they'd threatened to exert considerable pressure on his testicles unless he paid his gambling debts in full. But Colin didn't know any of this; he thought Alex just needed cheering up again.

'What's happening? Anything good?'

'I've got some papers for you to sign,' Alex said, gloomily.

'When?'

'Smedley's been asking about you, so come after eight. He's going to the opera.'

Colin arrived at five past. Alex buzzed him in.

'Do you mind if I smoke?'

Alex shook his head. Colin opened the window and sparked up.

'What have you got?'

Alex retrieved some documents from a far shelf. 'This is the company.'

'When was it registered?'

'Nineteen eighty-four.'

'Eight years is enough.'

'I took the liberty of picking a trading name,' Alex said.

'What?'

'Horizon Developments.'

'I like it. Well done.' Colin is good at being encouraging.

'So who are we going to get to cook the books?' Colin asked.

'Don't you know someone?' Alex said, surprised.

'Not with a good name. We need a kosher letterhead.'

'I might know an accountant,' Alex said.

'How well do you know him?'

'I went to school with him.'

Colin laughed. 'Good school, was it, Eton?' Alex remained silent, perhaps ashamed.

'I take it you don't want the company in your real name.'

'Put me down as – Roy Collins.'

'Roy!?' Alex laughed mockingly. 'That's a bit gay, isn't it?'

'You can fuck off. It's my middle name.'

Alex passed Colin a pen and watched him labour over a false signature on the company documents. Alex wiped his moistening forehead. At that moment, they were definitely crossing the line.

'Is Roy Collins your usual alias?' Alex was clearly anxious.

'I don't have a usual alias. This is my first time.'

By the time Colin left Alex's office, it was dumping rain. He hurried diagonally across the street to his parked cab and swore loudly when he stepped into an unexpectedly deep puddle. His expletive drew the attention of a rushing pedestrian and a raised brolly to scope the foul mouth.

While Colin unlocked his taxi, he glanced up at Alex's office and saw someone looking down at him from one of the first-floor windows. It was Smedley. Colin was startled because he was supposed to be at the opera. As Smedley was staring directly at him, Colin decided ignoring him would look suspicious. Colin nodded good evening. Smedley didn't answer the gesture. He simply stared back, watching the rain paste Colin's fringe to his forehead. He was probably wondering why an important client was driving a bloody taxi.

AGE OF INNOCENCE

'Have you ever been to prison?' I asked Colin. He didn't answer me straight away; instead, he finished reading my version of the scene where he and Alex set up the fake company.

Then he said, in his own time, 'Alex asked me that.'

'I'm not surprised.'

I waited for an answer to my prison question. None came.

'Well?'

'I've been close,' he said. 'And I'm not getting any closer.'

That was no comfort.

'What does that mean?'

'I'm not going any closer.'

'Are you going to answer?' I was getting tired of

his cryptic games. 'This isn't going to work if I can't trust you.'

'You can trust me,' Colin insisted. 'It's innocent until caught, remember?'

I shook my head in frustration.

'You're just like him,' Colin said.

I was intrigued to know what a failed screenwriter and a Burmese gambler had in common.

'In what way?' I asked.

'He liked to think he was honourable.'

It was another cunning deflection, but I didn't want to talk about me.

'Let's stop bickering,' I said, regretting that I sounded like a schoolmarm. 'I'm getting a bit bogged down with how the mortgage worked.'

He explained:

'It's like a normal mortgage. When you buy a house, you go to a bank, prove your income and they lend you the money. It was the same for Horizon Developments – we made it look like a profitable company that could afford a hefty mortgage.

'Of course, no one doubted Alex, coz he worked for a respectable law firm. And any bank could see our company was successful on paper, plus the property deal was sound as well. The rent from the tenants easily covered the interest on the loan.

They couldn't have asked for more. We had NatWest, a triple-A-rated household name, as our tenant. It was beautiful.

'Obviously the bank didn't realise we were going to run away with their money. You see, when a bank lends a developer a lot of money to buy a building, they give it to the developer's lawyer first, and he's supposed to transfer it to the seller. Note the "supposed", because you can't do this scam any more. Too many people ran away with the money. The rules have changed and the banks now transfer the money straight to where it's supposed to end up.

'But before we could steal the money, we had to buy the building.'

OLIVER TWIST

Colin was driving Alex to the towers to make their offer when he broke the news about being spotted by Smedley. He hadn't wanted to spook Alex, but he had no choice: he had to find out whether Smedley had overheard their meeting.

'Smedley saw me getting in the cab last night.'

Alex became as jumpy as a sack of kittens. 'You're kidding?' He used his handkerchief to remove the instant sweat from his neck.

'I didn't see him on my way out. Did he say anything?' Colin said.

Alex shook his head. 'So he saw you in the taxi?' Alex had become whiny.

'So what if I own a taxi? So does Cubby Broccoli. It's not a problem. How's your friend with the books?'

'He'll do it,' Alex said, 'but he wants two thousand.'

'Shall we go fifty-fifty?'

Alex looked embarrassed. 'I'm a bit short right now.'

'Don't worry. I've got five hundred. I'll drive non-stop for the rest. Should have it in a few days.'

'Thanks,' Alex said, relieved.

'How you doing with the mortgage?'

'I've been to four banks and I've got their application forms,' Alex said, pleased with himself. 'If Speyhawk accept your offer, I'll apply.'

'Apply anyway. We haven't got time.'

Alex went silent.

'You all right?' Colin asked.

'I don't know whether I like all this any more.' Colin hates quitters; he ignored Alex to halt any more doubter's talk.

They finished the journey to King's Cross in silence. Colin parked the cab around the corner from the towers to avoid being seen as the driver.

'Here we go,' Colin said to gee himself up, and then he trod out his cigarette.

Alex pulled himself together and surprised Colin with an upbeat offer. 'I'll do all the talking, if you like. It'll give you some gravitas.'

Colin smiled at Alex's change of mood and set

off, leading the way up the steep steps to the main tower's front door. Waiting for them at the top was the estate agent, or Commercial Agent as his business card said. He was The Toff, the badly dressed drunk from whom Colin had overheard the tip in the first place. I can't describe what he was wearing because Colin only said it was bloody awful.

The agent greeted Colin with an outstretched hand and expansive grin. Colin was confident the agent wouldn't remember him: the last time they'd met, The Toff was pissed, he'd only been looking at the back of Colin's head and it was dark. Nevertheless, Colin was relieved to note that The Toff showed no sign of recognition.

'Mr Collins?' Someone had told the agent that good salesmen always maintain eye contact; he fixed Colin with a superglue stare.

'Are you the agent?' Colin said, immediately taking charge of the meeting – much to Alex's anger; he started sweating even more.

'I've got my lawyer here coz I want to be quick.'

The agent shook Alex's hand. 'We all want to be quick, Mr Collins.'

'I don't need to look round,' Colin said. 'I've seen the rental contract and that's enough for me.'

'Right,' said the agent.

'What do they want for it?' Colin asked.

'What's your offer?' Ding ding. The bout had begun.

'What do they want?' Colin asked, refusing to say the first figure. His father had drummed it into him: the man who says the first figure loses.

'Well, as we're all in a hurry, I know they'll take eighty.'

'Fifty,' Colin said, remembering the figure he'd overheard.

'Mr Collins, the building's a bargain at eighty.'

'Not if you need to sell in a hurry.'

'This isn't a fire sale, Mr Collins.'

'Oh really? I think we can both smell smoke.'

'What do you mean?'

'I have it on good authority from a very reliable source that Speyhawk are a little hot under the collar.'

'They'll want more than fifty to cool them down.'

'Of course they will. But that's all I'm offering.'

The agent shook his head for dramatic effect.

'Look,' Colin said. 'I've looked at the rent and it only supports fifty. I'm not trying to insult anyone. I'm being up front.'

'They might consider sixty.'

Colin gritted his teeth. 'If they want to play games, let's call it forty.'

The agent was amazed by Colin's tactic.

'I'm sorry, Mr Collins.' The agent turned and walked away. He was playing the double bluff. Colin stayed rooted to the spot. Alex started to go after the agent.

'Stay still,' Colin hissed at Alex.

Eight paces later, the agent turned – like a duellist, Colin said – and fired his last shot.

'Can you complete by the end of next week?'

Alex looked nervous. That only gave them ten days to find a bank and raise fifty million pounds.

'No problem,' Colin said.

'Ten days?' Alex said, the pitch of his voice changing sharply as he stopped himself from squealing.

Colin ignored Alex and offered the agent his hand.

'I'll put it to them,' the agent said.

'Give the answer to Alex. Alex, give the man your card.'

Alex did as he was told. Colin noticed the agent was suddenly studying him closely. Fearing the agent might have recognised him, Colin beat him to it with, 'Have we met before?'

'I was just wondering that,' the agent said.

'Well, property's a small world. If we have, good to meet you again. Until next time.'

They all shook hands and parted company.

Colin was delighted. The agent was just about satisfied. Alex was livid.

When they got to the taxi, Alex exploded.

'I thought I said I'd do the talking.'

Colin turned on him. 'Don't be soft, Alex. If he don't think I've got the balls, he won't take me seriously.'

'This isn't a game, you know,' Alex said.

'It is now.'

Alex went silent.

'What's your problem, Alex? I got the right price, didn't I?'

'And you think we can get a fifty-million loan by next Friday?'

Colin didn't relent. 'You'll have to.'

THE SHIPPING NEWS

Alex raised his game over the next ten days. The loan application was approved easily, but Colin wasn't surprised because he had faith in Alex's thoroughness and, more importantly, he knew the building's income easily covered the mortgage. Any bank would have assessed it as a risk-free loan. In fact, if Colin hadn't instinctively been a con man, the deal would have turned him into a very successful commercial landlord.

Alex also scored highly with Margot, certainly impressing her more than Colin had expected. Alex had contacted her to arrange a meeting. She, like many American tourists, had been charmed by his just darling Georgian office and she just adored the thought of the commission she'd earn. The real Margot was a woman of considerable appetite. In her long and varied international career, she'd already tried Chinese and Thai; luckily for Alex, she wasn't going to say no to a bit of Burmese. It turned out Margot was more than happy to mix business with pleasure. In fact, she was in business for the pleasure.

Thus invigorated, Margot returned home to Amsterdam and chose for Alex's supposed client a selection of diamonds worth fifty million pounds: nothing too large, nothing over five carats (so they'd be easy to cash in) and nothing without a certificate of authentication. She enjoyed selecting so many diamonds and arranged for them to be collected from a bonded warehouse at Schiphol Airport on the outskirts of Amsterdam. The plan was straightforward: once she was paid for the diamonds, she'd release the bond – a grand name but just a stamped piece of paper – that allowed the bearer to collect them from Schiphol. All Alex had to do was transfer the fifty-million loan to Margot's account.

Everything was set. Everything was shiny.

Then Smedley slithered into Alex's office. It was the night before the transfer day. Smedley was in a dinner jacket and just about to leave for the opera he'd missed the week before when he saw the light in Alex's office. He poked his head round the door without knocking. Smedley was a fan of old-fashioned grooming and his pomade lent his hair the sheen of a cheap coffin.

'Your new client,' he said, startling Alex, who decided to avoid covering his papers in case the action looked suspect.

'Sorry, sir?'

'Is he a *taxi driver*?' Smedley said it with the revulsion of a man tasting a sheep's eye for the first time.

Alex had to think fast. Fortunately, he remembered a conversation when he and Colin had been discussing cars. Colin had said that even if he could afford any car in the world, he'd still choose a taxi because a taxi can be parked anywhere in London – for free.

'He's very mean,' Alex said.

'What?'

'He doesn't like paying for parking. So he bought a taxi so he can park for free. He's a bit eccentric, you see.'

'So which is he? Mean – or eccentric?' Smedley clearly wasn't convinced.

'Both,' Alex said.

'How convenient.'

Then Smedley checked his watch. 'I'm late, but we'll talk more about your tight twit tomorrow.' Smedley was delighted by his spontaneous alliteration and Alex heard him tittering all the way down the stairs. Alex calmed himself with the thought it would be the last time he'd ever have to listen to Smedley.

WAITING TO EXHALE

The next day – transfer day – Alex decided the best way to avoid Smedley was to avoid the office altogether. Instead, he went straight to the firm's bank, the Midland Bank, now HSBC, on the corner of Poultry, a briefly named but still lavish street in the City. The bank has a facia hewn from a Portland quarry and is a particularly grand affair designed by Edwin Lutyens, the architect also responsible for the Cenotaph in Whitehall. Alex liked the bank and knew it well. Although he was junior in the firm, he dealt with the client account often. He would volunteer to go to the bank in person because it was his refuge from his mean-spirited office. Apart from the comfortable chill of the marbled interior in summer, he especially liked the warm way the bank staff treated him. His firm was a major client, and the tellers always accorded him the respect of assumed high association. Visiting the bank gave him the opportunity to enjoy a little authority, if only for the time it took for his place in the queue to expire. He wasn't confident of much in life, but he was confident there would be no problem with the bank, even for such a large sum.

The money was due to hit the firm's account at midday. Alex and Colin met outside the bank at ten to. While Colin waited in the ticking-over taxi, hardly the fastest of getaway cars, Alex went into the bank and remembered to keep his shoulders back in front of the staff. He joined a line of one by the personal accounts desk and was soon seated opposite a new woman whom he didn't recognise. This threw him more than he was expecting, but he took a breath and calmly explained he'd phoned ahead to warn that the firm's client account would be receiving fifty million pounds sterling. The assistant was less patient than her colleagues and asked him in a brusque tone to speak up, which he did, but only a little as the bank's marble interior had a magnifying acoustic. He told her he needed to transfer the fifty million to Holland straight away. He handed over a letter of authorisation on the firm's expensive cream stationery, which carried

Edward Smedley's signature. It was a good forgery: Alex had practised it as eagerly as a teenager dreaming of autograph hunters.

While the assistant checked the console on her desk, Alex waited patiently, hoping nobody noticed he was rubbing his sweaty palms on his trousers.

'It's not in yet,' he told Colin outside. Alex's sweat was flowing freely now. Colin got out of the cab and lit a cigarette.

'Can I have one, please?' asked Alex.

'You don't smoke,' said Colin with a parental bark.

Alex checked his watch. 'They're nearly twenty minutes late.'

'Let's check again,' ordered Colin.

Colin took the lead and marched into the bank. Alex beat him to the personal accounts desk, where a lunchtime queue had developed. An old woman ahead of them took an age to settle her half-moons and then even longer to create an elaborate signature.

When she was finally finished, Alex approached the desk for his turn, but it was now a different assistant. Their simple plan had failed to allow for something as simple as a lunch hour. Alex had to explain it all again – without sweating.

Some minutes later, the assistant said, 'No.' And then she got up from her desk. 'But I'll just check on the mainframe, sir. It's more up to date.' She left Alex waiting and he wiped his palms again.

Colin, loitering nearby, looked at his watch. Alex looked at the door. Then he gulped. He signalled to Colin, who noticed Alex was wearing the stare of a delicate child on a first visit to the snake house. Smedley had just walked in. Alex tried to hide his face behind one of the bank's promotional leaflets. Colin moved away from Alex.

By the time Smedley noticed Alex, Colin had managed to hide behind a pillar. As Smedley homed in on Alex, Colin took advantage of the distraction to slip out of the bank; Alex would have had a lot of explaining to do if Smedley had seen Colin in the firm's bank.

'What are you doing here?' Smedley asked, with a snarl.

Alex thought fast. 'I bank here myself. I thought I'd take an early lunch.'

'Did you indeed? Well, hurry up. I'll see you in my office later. You and I need to have a talk.'

'Yes, sir,' Alex said, his head approaching a bow. Fortunately for Alex, Smedley then became aware of all the other customers scowling at him for queue-jumping. He left Alex alone and went to the back of the line.

Just then, the bank assistant returned.

'It's in, Mister Warwick.'

Alex sighed with relief and pulled the chair closer. He lowered his voice, acutely aware that Smedley was staring at his every move. Alex took the transfer authorisation from his inside pocket and slid it, still unfolded, over to the assistant. He hoped Smedley wouldn't recognise the distinctive colour of the company stationery. While he waited for the assistant to finish typing, Alex turned to look over his shoulder at Smedley, who leered back a false smile.

'There we are, sir,' said the assistant to Alex. 'The transfer's complete.'

Alex turned to smile at Smedley for the last time.

Outside, Colin was pacing around his taxi. A policeman walked over and looked Colin up and down. In his suit, Colin didn't look like a cab driver.

'Where's the driver?' the cop asked.

'In the bank.'

'The cab's illegally parked.'

'I'll tell him,' Colin said.

'I'll be back in five minutes.'

'See you later.'

The policeman kept an eye on Colin, who

decided to move the taxi round the corner where it would be safer. It was only a matter of minutes since Colin had left Alex. Then Colin saw Smedley coming out of the bank. Colin ducked down behind the cab.

When he guessed the coast was clear, Colin ran across the street and into the bank. Alex wasn't there. He rushed back outside, but there was no sign of him.

GONE WITH THE WIND

Colin's escape plan was simple. They would take a train to the ferry and then cab it to Amsterdam. Colin chose the train, ferry and cab because they could pay cash and thus minimise their trail. They avoided flying because their passports might be noted and they wanted no one to know where they were going. And people would have been looking, because when you've just nicked fifty million quid, they always do.

As soon as Colin discovered Alex was no longer in the bank, he thought of the next stage in the plan and drove to Liverpool Street train station. He dumped the taxi at the far end of a rank, where it wouldn't be in the way or draw attention to itself, and sprinted across the concourse to the information board. Because of his dyslexia, he couldn't read it properly, but he asked a guard for the train to Harwich in Essex. It was leaving in three minutes. The barrier was closing in two.

Colin dashed to platform seven and side-stepped the ticket inspector. He hurried down the platform with everyone else who was rushing for the train. As he couldn't get on unless Alex was on it, he peered through every window hoping to see his missing partner. Nothing. He was nearly at the end of the train when he realised he'd ignored the first-class carriage at the front, all the way back up the platform.

The last door was being slammed shut when he saw Alex sitting under the first-class sign. Alex beamed at Colin like a child who'd spotted Santa. Colin had yet to find out what a good actor his partner was.

Alex caused a stir by rushing through the carriage to open the door for his lost partner.

'Where the fuck did you get to?' Colin said.

'Where did *you* get to? Smedley wanted me to wait, but I used the other door to get out. Your cab was gone, so I cabbed it straight here.'

Colin shook his head at the ridiculous confusion. They'd missed each other by seconds. Alex started to giggle.

As the train pulled away from the station, they

settled into their first-class seats and discussed for the first time, with a few laughs, their different encounters with Margot.

'Do I really have to see her again?' Alex asked, wincing.

'Whatever it takes,' Colin said with a smile.

FROM HERE TO ETERNITY

They caught the Harwich ferry to the Hook of Holland as foot passengers with plenty of time to spare, and when they got there, had an hour-long cab journey to Margot's office in Amsterdam.

En route to Margot, Colin stopped for a generous horde of lilies as a thank-you present. While he hid outside, Alex swapped the bouquet for the bond and the keys to the hire car she'd arranged for him. As Margot had no idea Colin had been anything more than an introduction, she didn't guess he was on her doorstep.

It was evening by then and Alex was a little delayed when Margot invited him in for a drink. As Alex was eager to collect the diamonds, he soon made his excuses to Margot and they double air-kissed goodbye.

It was late by the time they got to the bonded warehouse at Schiphol Airport. Colin parked in the shadows and they kept their heads bowed walking across the car park for fear of being recorded by the myriad of security cameras. The Dutch guard authenticated the bond. Colin was amused to find the vault was like a scene from a heist movie. When he unwrapped the first black velvet parcel of diamonds, he smiled in sheer admiration.

'Nice to meet you,' he whispered, caressing the gently clicking handful.

On the road, clear of the security cameras and now with a precious briefcase in the footwell at Alex's feet, they allowed themselves an air-punching scream of celebration.

'Well done, son,' Colin shouted, slapping Alex on the shoulder.

An hour later, they'd cleared the city and were following the moon across Holland's famously horizontal landscape, past silhouettes of windmills against a full-moon sky. Professional drivers like Colin drive by instinct. They never notice when they're checking their mirrors, which they do often. On maybe the hundredth check, Colin noticed the silver Jag. There was no traffic and the empty road drew attention to the headlights behind them. Colin wouldn't have been suspicious had he not noticed the British number plates. He sped up to check whether they were following. The Jag sped up as well. He didn't realise they'd been trailed since Alex boarded the Harwich train. What had been a relaxed escape for Colin had given Alex's pursuers all the time they needed to drive their car on to the ferry and follow them to Amsterdam.

'We've got company,' he told Alex, who spun round nervously in his seat. Colin slammed his foot on the accelerator and the hire car took off. It raced to one hundred and eighty kilometres per hour.

'Do you know them?' Colin asked calmly.

'No,' Alex said quickly. Too quickly, Colin thought.

Colin pressed the accelerator, but he was already on the floor. He checked his mirror. The Jag had gone. Colin's pace had bought them a quarter of a mile.

Suddenly, Colin slammed on the brakes and did a screeching one-eighty in the empty road. Then he started hurrying back the way they'd come: back towards the Jag.

'What are you doing?' Alex screamed.

'Who are they?' Colin said.

The road straightened ahead of them and they could see the Jag coming towards them. Impact was ten seconds away.

'Tell me the truth,' Colin said, still calm.

'I don't know,' Alex screamed. 'Turn round!'

'Tell me the truth.' Colin moved the Merc into the oncoming lane. Alex shrieked. Colin was playing chicken – clearly determined to hit the Jag unless Alex told him the truth. Blinding headlights filled the windscreen. A crash was inevitable. Alex gripped the dashboard, arms locked, bracing for impact. Three. Two. One.

Alex shouted, 'I know them!'

The jag flinched first. Colin yanked the wheel to twitch his car out of its way. Metal blurred. Lights streaked. Brakes shrieked. The Jag swerved off the tarmac. Colin wrestled with his skidding car. The Jag lurched into a roadside canal. Meanwhile, Colin had to use the full width of the road to stop.

Colin glanced across at the Jag. The nose was drowning in the mud. The ongoing momentum of its sudden halt had lifted the back; the Jag was angled almost upright like a crooked head-stone.

Colin turned to Alex. An empty stillness had filled the cabin. They were strangers again. Alex was staring straight ahead, denying eye contact.

'I thought you were a fucking gentleman,' Colin said bitterly.

Alex turned away and found himself facing the knotted underbelly of the steaming, leaking Jag.

'Who are they?' Colin said.

'I owe them money,' Alex whispered.

'How much?'

'Over a million.'

'Fucking hell! What for? Drugs?'

'Gambling.'

'Why didn't you tell me? We could've sorted something out.'

Silence.

Then Alex opened the door ajar and plunged his face towards the tarmac. The sound of bilious retching was accompanied by the instant cabin light that threw an unwelcome glow over the arched back of Colin's furtive partner.

'I know how you feel,' Colin said.

Colin checked the Jag again, but no one was stirring. He looked at his watch. It was late, but he scanned the mirrors in case anyone else was on the road. Nothing. Colin lit a cigarette. While Alex's pitiful groaning got on his nerves, Colin watched greedy bugs dive-bomb the unseen windscreen.

Finally, Alex dragged himself upright and wiped his mouth. 'Let's go,' he said.

'Who put you in charge?'

'We can't hang around,' Alex shouted patronisingly, as if goading Colin.

Colin nodded at the Jag. 'See if they're dead.'

'I can't.' Alex whimpered like a child. One second he was tough, then he was wet. Colin couldn't stand the indecision. He snuffed the engine and took the keys for good measure.

He prowled over to the Jag, keeping his distance in case they sprang out. When he saw they were both still, he moved closer. He prepared himself for gruesome detail. It was better than he'd feared. Both heads were slumped forward. The driver had blond hair and an untamed fringe. The passenger shaved his own head and couldn't reach the neckline to do a very good job. They were both unconscious, but Colin could see no blood. Their torsos were suspended by their seatbelts – like paratroopers in a forest – but they were still breathing. Colin was grateful not to be a murderer on top of everything else that had gone wrong. Both started to stir and would soon come round.

Then Colin heard the engine. The Merc's engine.

He spun round and saw Alex's silhouette on the driver's side. He must have arranged for a spare key.

Everything zoomed into slomo. The brake light

died as the handbrake was released. The white reverse light flashed on and off as the automatic gear selector slid past reverse and on to drive. And then the back tyres were spinning and billowing smoke.

Colin snapped into action and sprinted after him. Within seconds, he was getting closer to the Merc. He was only ten feet away. Then five. He could almost feel the greasy chrome of the door handle. But three feet was the closest he got. Then it was double figures. And then it was triple. It was no use. It was over. He'd lost the race before the gun had even gone off. If only he'd had a gun.

The silver Merc was soon on the black horizon. There was one last flash of red as Alex touched the brakes to round the last corner. And then he was gone. And so were the diamonds. For ever.

Colin stood abandoned in the middle of the road. He'd been completely outmanoeuvred. If he went to the police, he'd be arrested. To trace Alex, he'd need Smedley – who'd turn him in. Even to trace the hire car, he'd need Margot and that would mean confessing his involvement, and if she found out her diamonds were paid for with stolen money, she'd turn him in. Alex had been in charge all along. He'd thought of everything. And he'd made sure Colin had nothing.

THE HITCHHIKER'S GUIDE TO THE GALAXY

I watched Colin read the scene where Alex ran off with the diamonds and saw his jaw clench.

'The little bastard,' he couldn't help blurting out.

'So you didn't go after him?' I said.

'What could I do?' It was the first time I'd heard defeat in Colin's voice. 'I couldn't dig too much without falling in myself.'

When Alex failed to transfer the money to Speyhawk on time, their lawyers immediately called Roy Collins' lawyers, namely Alex's office. Smedley took the call, but there was nothing he could do to cover for his fraudulent employee. Not having a spare fifty million pounds, he turned to the Law Society, the body that governs the activities of all UK solicitors. The Law Society makes it their business to safeguard the trustworthy reputation of all British solicitors by insuring against the malpractice of any of its members. They guarantee that even the rotten apples will be palatable.

As Alex would have known the police were looking for him, he definitely would have stayed away from England, not least because he hated the place.

'He's probably in some Rangoon casino right now, putting my money on the table,' Colin said jealously. 'And I'm back in the cab.'

'What about his gambling debts?'

'He must've paid them coz they never came after me. He could afford it – with my share in his pocket.'

Colin couldn't bear the memories any longer and changed the subject. 'So, what's the ending?' he said.

'You've just said it,' I said.

'What?'

'You're back in the cab.'

'What are we saying here? Crime doesn't pay? Am I a vicar all of a sudden?'

'The story comes full circle,' I said. 'You start in the taxi and finish in the taxi.'

'When will it be done?' he asked as if ordering a takeaway.

'Tomorrow.' I enjoyed sounding decisive for once.

'Then what do we do with it?' he said casually. I was amazed he asked that.

'You give it to Mr Hollywood, of course.' I was annoyed I had to explain the obvious.

'What Mr Hollywood?' he said, treating me like the fool.

'Mr If-You're-Any-Good-You'll-Find-Me.'

'But I don't know who he is,' he said.

'What?' I'd raised my voice.

'I told you, I don't know anything about the movie business.'

'Are you telling me I've just spent the last four months writing a script for a Hollywood hotshot you can't even get to?'

'I never said I knew who he was,' Colin said. 'I just told you he was rich, he said it was a good story and I should get it written down.'

I was stunned. I'd assumed Colin knew who he was, but he had no idea. I'd been seduced by the thought of easy access to Hollywood. I'd been a fool.

'You've conned me. I was going to write it and you were going to sell it to Hollywood. I knew I shouldn't have trusted you.' I was surprised by my directness.

Colin looked shocked. Then I felt ashamed of

my insult and tried to find a solution to our predicament.

'Sorry. What did he look like?'

'He had a beard.'

I had to laugh.

'What's so funny?' he said.

'They all have beards: Spielberg, Scorsese, Coppola, George Lucas, James Cameron . . .'

'And glasses,' he added, trying to be helpful. That wasn't even funny.

'We're never going to find him,' I said.

'You must know some people,' he said.

'No one who'll take me seriously. I told you, I've never sold anything.' I immediately resented my beaten tone. 'And anyway, you're supposed to be selling it.'

Silence.

I tried to imagine how my brilliant father would handle the crisis. Then I remembered how Colin had met both the mystery man and me.

'How did you meet me?' I asked, taking charge.

'You got in my cab,' he said, confused as I obviously knew the answer.

'How did you meet Alex? And learn about the building?'

'In the *cab*.' He smiled. He'd got it. 'It's the key.'

'Now. Where did you meet your friend with the beard?'

'Wardour Street.'

'You're going to have to network this, Colin,' I said, impressed by my new-found authority.

'What do you mean?'

'We know you can meet people in the cab. All you've got to do is be in the right place.'

'Where's that?'

'Soho.'

INTERVIEW WITH THE VAMPIRE

One of the perks of writing a script is you get to type THE END on the last page. Poets don't sign off with so satisfying a flourish. Nor novelists. Nor journalists. It's the one bonus of being a screenwriter. Typing THE END is an unnecessary indulgence because you've obviously got there. It's childish and gratifying, but ultimately untrue. It's a momentary sense of completion and, indeed, the only sense of completion most screenwriters ever feel. Because, unlike the output of the other forms of writing listed above, a script – never a screenplay, which is considered a rookie phrase – is nothing in itself, just an instruction manual for a story. It isn't the work itself, just a guide to what the finished film might be. On completion, a poet has a poem, a novelist has a novel and a journalist has an article; whereas the screenwriter has just one hundred and twenty pages with words typed on them. The truth is: when a screenwriter types THE END, it's really the beginning. Because, until a script is transformed into a film, it's nothing. Ironically, when it becomes a film, the script goes back to being nothing because you've got the film. And once you've got the film, you don't need the script. After all, once you've assembled a flat-pack wardrobe, you no longer need the instructions.

Nonetheless, we needed some flat-pack instructions and I ended ours like this:

CUT TO:

147. EXT. LIVERPOOL STREET STATION — NIGHT

Colin walks slowly across the empty platform to the taxi rank outside. It's raining. His taxi sits alone where he parked it not even twenty-four hours earlier. He searches his pockets and finds his key in the last one. Reluctantly, he unlocks the cab.

He heaves himself behind the wheel and starts the engine. He pauses for a moment, clearly unhappy to be listening to the relentless grind of the diesel engine; he's back to square one.

Then, with a decisive breath, he turns on the FOR HIRE sign, checks the mirror and with the hint of a smile drives into the night — to find his next passenger.

FADE TO BLACK

THE END

I was particularly relieved to type the last two words. And then I realised we didn't have a title.

'What shall we call it?' I asked Colin over the phone.

He thought for a moment and then announced grandly, 'The Optimist.'

'That's a bit Waltons, isn't it?'

'What do you mean?'

'The Optimist is a bit, you know, sweet. A bit girly.'

'You can fuck off,' he said.

'How about The Opportunist?' I said.

I think he was flattered my word wasn't so far from his.

'I like it,' he said. 'Well done.'

I typed a front cover, ran the spellchecker, saved it, saved it again, ink-jetted a master copy, checked no pages were missing, enjoyed the weight of my work and, later that afternoon, handed it to Colin in a pristine envelope. I'd hoped for a sense of ceremony, but he didn't hang around. He was eager to hit his new target: Soho, London's film capital. He went straight off to get the script photocopied. I went straight to bed.

The phone woke me. It was dark outside; I'd slept all afternoon.

'Hello,' I said loudly, knowing volume was the only way I'd instantly clear my throat and avoid sounding sleepy.

'Been asleep?' Colin asked. He didn't wait for an answer.

'This fella gets in the cab,' he said, 'and we get talking. "What do you do for a living?" I say. He says he makes films. "What's your name?" I say. "Neil Jordan," he says . . .'

'Hang on, Colin. *Who* did you say?' I was so excited I wanted to hear it again just to eke out the good news.

'Neil Jordan.'

'Do you know who Neil Jordan is?'

I was amazed.

'Yeah, he's a scruffy paddy who just got in the

back of my cab.' Colin was delighted by his cheek.

'Do you know what he directed? *Mona Lisa, Michael Collins, Interview With the Vampire, The Crying Game* . . .'

'He'll do,' he said, chirpily.

'What did he say?'

'He writes his own stuff, but he'll take a look.'

'Well done, Colin.'

'I've got his number. I'll call him tomorrow.'

'No, Colin. Give him a chance to read it.'

'How long?'

'A week at least.' What did I know?

'Not a bad start, hey?' He laughed. 'Now, you go to bed. I'm going to Soho.'

VANITY FAIR

I woke the next morning having dreamt about Bob Hoskins. This strange confession is probably explained by his starring role as a driver in Neil Jordan's moving film *Mona Lisa*. I don't want to push the explanation too far because *Mona Lisa* is also about lesbian prostitutes. Anyway, I phoned Colin and suggested Bob Hoskins would be a good taxi-driving con man. Hoskins was a truly excellent tough but vulnerable gangster in *The Long Good Friday*. Colin doesn't understand concepts like vulnerable, but we did agree that John Mackenzie's film was one of the best gangster movies ever set in London.

'But he doesn't look anything like me,' Colin said.

'Colin, this isn't about you any more.'

'What do you mean?'

'We're not doing the life and times of Colin Hayday. It's a story,' I said.

'But he's too short. And he's hairy.'

'Forget this is based on you. You've got to think about British actors who are big in Hollywood. Bob Hoskins was in *Roger Rabbit*. He may be short. But he's *huge*.' I enjoyed talking about films with Colin. It was the only time I had more experience than him.

'Hang on,' Colin said. 'Sammy can get to Bob Hoskins.'

'Who's Sammy?'

'Sammy Pasha. He's his PA – sometimes drives him. I'll give him a call.'

'You're very well connected,' I said, impressed.

'No, I'm not. He's all I've got.'

But it did partially make up for not delivering his bearded admirer from Hollywood.

Colin moved fast. By the time I'd put the kettle on, he'd phoned Sammy and by the time it had boiled, Colin had called me back to say Sammy would do it.

'I need another script,' demanded Colin.

'What happened to the master copy?'

'I gave it to Neil Jordan.'

Colin handed a script to Sammy, who kindly said

he'd give it to Bob Hoskins. Sammy was doing us an enormous favour because stars hate to be hassled, but, by coincidence, Sammy was picking up Bob Hoskins from the airport the next day. I couldn't believe it. This was easy. Neil Jordan, a director I admired enormously, was reading my script and so was a hot actor who just happened to have worked with Jordan in a successful film I also admired. The omens looked good.

That night, the phone rang. It was Colin.

'I pick up this lady, right,' he launched in without saying hello. 'I ask if she does anything interesting and she says she's an agent. Her name's Jenne Casarotto. Guess who she represents?'

'Who?' I was jumping up and down.

'Only Neil Jordan,' Colin said casually.

'No!' It was too incredible a coincidence.

'I told her to tell him to hurry up and read the script.'

'Colin! You can't tell these people what to do.'

'If you don't tell people what you want, you don't get,' he said.

A week later, Colin called again. It was rudely late.

'Did I wake you?' he said.

'No,' I said, trying to swallow a yawn.

'I've just called Neil Jordan.' No!

'It's nearly midnight!'

'I couldn't wait.'

'What did he say?' I couldn't wait either.

'He said he likes it, but he's doing his own script. He says he'd pass. What does that mean?'

I was instantly flat. 'Pass means no. It means unfortunately.'

'But he likes it,' Colin said.

'Not enough.' I wondered whether Colin hounding him and his agent had anything to do with the rejection.

A week later, waiting in the postal cowpat on my welcome mat was a letter from Bob Hoskins's agent. I couldn't believe it: there was an 'Unfortunately' at the start of line three. Mr Hoskins was too busy in Hollywood to consider any UK projects. A week before, we'd had the chance of everything. Now, we had an unfortunate nothing.

'We're back to square one,' I moaned to Colin.

'He was too short anyway,' Colin said. 'But don't worry. We've still got Neil Jordan.'

'No we haven't.'

'He said he likes it.'

'He was only being polite.'

'We don't have to tell people that.'

I knew there was no point trying to control Colin. I wouldn't be in the cab to stop him saying exactly what he wanted. Maybe I didn't want to stop him – because it was the closest I'd been to getting a film made. It was already uncomfortable. But I couldn't complain because I had chosen to work with a con man. I had chosen to get real.

WHO'S AFRAID OF VIRGINIA WOOLF?

Colin continued to target Soho and, despite my warning, I know he was hinting to every passenger that Neil Jordan might be interested in directing his film. He told everyone that Jordan had the script, which was still true, but he omitted to say he'd 'passed' on it.

This illusion of approval by a top director probably helped him to win over – let's call her Virginia. It's a good Sloaney name and Colin said she was 'a classic Sloane'. We can say she worked for September Films, the big London production company. Virginia liked the story Colin told her in the cab and asked to see the script. She read it quickly and called Colin, suggesting they meet in Soho Square.

'She wants to talk about the rights,' Colin told me over the phone. I was so excited I didn't think to ask why I wasn't invited to the meeting.

Soho Square is one of only a few patches of grass left in central London and is consequently a magnet for the postcode's lunchtime sun-worshippers. Colin met Virginia well after lunch and they managed to find an empty bench among the prostrate couriers and their reclining racing bikes. She tested a scalding cappuccino while Colin tinged the ring pull on the day's fifth Coke.

'You read it quick. You must like it.' Colin was forcing the pace.

'It's a great story,' she said.

'You said something about an option. What's that?'

'An option is when you give us the exclusive option to develop the film, usually for a year or two. We pay you, of course.'

'How much?'

'We'll come to that.'

'So what happens next?' Colin was running before she wanted to walk.

'We want to use our writer,' she said bluntly, realising this was the only way to deal with Colin.

'Why?'

'Well, no one knows your writer.'

'Who've you got? William Shakespeare?'

'It's just that we're used to our writer.'

'Well, I'm not. What would I tell my guy? Sorry, mate, it's curtains?'

'Look, Colin, this is pretty common stuff.'

'What? You read something you like and then bin the guy who wrote it?' Colin was getting angry. Virginia was probably grateful she'd chosen a public place for the meeting.

Colin came to the flat to tell me what had happened.

'So what did they say?' I asked at the door eagerly. 'What did they offer?'

'A quid,' Colin said quietly.

'A pound?' I didn't mean to sound as if I was correcting him.

'She said they'd offer one pound to option the rights. They'd develop the film themselves.'

He went silent.

'And what did *you* say?' I was tunnelling with a spoon.

Colin took a breath. 'I said thank you, but no thank you.'

I was stunned; I'd been tunnelling *into* prison. 'You said no to them developing the film?'

Colin hadn't told me about the other writer.

'You idiot!' I screamed. 'You should have taken the option.'

'There was nothing to take,' Colin shouted back. 'They were going to do it their way and give us zilch. Fuck 'em.'

'The point is, it would have been a start,' I said.

Colin clearly couldn't understand the importance of this to me.

'They were only going to give us a quid. That's the fucking point,' he said.

I got angry.

'The point is,' I shouted and then forced myself to calm my voice. 'The point is, you could have – *asked* – *me* – *first*. I thought we were in this fifty-fifty.'

Colin took out some change and flicked a silver coin across the room. I was pleased I managed to catch it.

'Well, there's fifty pence,' he said. 'Consider yourself paid in full.'

I was about to launch into an attack on Colin's manifest obsession with money, but my manners dragged me back. And it would have been pointless. My silence sparked some humility in Colin.

'Look, I'm sorry,' he said quietly. 'I had no choice.'

'Forget it,' I said begrudgingly, wishing he'd just go.

'I didn't want to tell you this,' he said, ignoring the instant curiosity of my eye contact. 'They wanted to bring in their writer.'

I tried to sidestep the first punch of humiliation. 'As a co-writer?' I whispered desperately, as if having the conversation quietly would lessen its impact.

'No.'

He didn't need to explain further. I nodded shamefully. I knew my script hadn't been good enough, and I knew the fault was all mine. I had to accept every bit of blame. I also knew he'd stopped them from insulting me any further. At last I had a reason to trust him. He could have gone with them, but he'd looked out for me instead. I should have been pleased, been reassured by Colin's first hint of loyalty. But I was all-consumed by my failure.

'Well, if you'll excuse me, I'd better get on with a rewrite,' I said. 'I hate the scene where Colin meets his partner.' I didn't mean it to sound as if I was saying I wished *we'd* never become partners, but I think that's how he took it. He said nothing more and left. I don't know who was more upset that night: me for feeling my script was utterly useless or Colin for suspecting his partner loathed him.

THE HOUND OF
THE BASKERVILLES

While I stayed at home, incessantly rewriting the script, Colin went back to work. He always did. It was his way of dealing with failure. He was looking for an opportunity to replace the one he'd lost. No matter where his journeys took him, he returned to Soho.

He was driving down Oxford Street in the rain, a time when cabs become as popular as Fridays, when an old man with a dog hailed the cab. The man was called Dennis Selinger. I don't know the dog's name. The dog wasn't important – because the man was an agent. And not just any old agent: an ICM agent. Those initials stand for International Creative Management. ICM were the undisputed number-one actors' agents in the world, the human staples that bound the deals that made Hollywood's biggest films. ICM were the big initials until CAA (Creative Artists Agency) came along to share the perch. All the big agents now go by initials and one of those initials is usually a C because they like to flatter their clients that they're Creative and that it's about more than just the Money.

In the universe of agents, Dennis Selinger was considered a planet. He represented proper Hollywood stars such as Marlon Brando, Michael Caine and Omar Sharif. Dennis liked Colin's pitch and agreed to a meeting. I was pleased because Colin told me he'd arranged it for both of us. Colin was learning, or at least teaching himself. He didn't want me to accuse him again of not doing things fifty-fifty.

Colin and I met at ICM's London office in Oxford Street. I wore a charcoal suit. So did Colin. We looked like a pair of roof tiles. We introduced ourselves to the immaculate receptionist and were invited to sit down. I overheard the receptionist phoning Dennis and then she came over and offered us a drink. That was a bad sign. Dennis had probably told her to stall us. When you see people drinking in reception, you know they're not important; important people are shown straight in. Only losers are kept waiting.

I asked for coffee and Colin went for tea. He did his dreadfully grating 'two sugars, stirred once to the left' line, which baffled the receptionist, but she continued smiling anyway. I wondered what Dennis was doing. Maybe he was taking a conference call from Brando. Maybe, if I listened carefully, I'd hear the Godfather slurping ice cream. Apparently Marlon ate several tubs a day. I was wondering what flavour was his favourite when a disinterested assistant appeared.

'Mr Selinger will see you now.'

Colin wisely abandoned his tea in reception, but I didn't want to appear ungrateful and carried my half-finished cup down a long corridor until we arrived at the inner sanctum, Dennis's corner office. The assistant stepped aside for us by the door and Colin and I had a ridiculous manners battle, each inviting the other to go first. The assistant clearly wasn't impressed by our inflated show of courtesy. Eventually I let Colin win and walked in first.

The meeting didn't start well. Dennis obviously wasn't expecting me.

'Colin, good to see you again,' he said – to me – as I swapped my coffee cup and offered my hand. I put his confusion down to old age or maybe the fact that he'd only seen the back of Colin's head when they'd first met in the taxi.

I was about to introduce myself when Colin's mitt shot past me to greet Dennis's outstretched hand. Dennis effortlessly hid his mistake by blanking me completely and changing his attention exclusively to Colin.

'Nice to see you, Dennis. How's business?' Colin sounded impressively familiar.

'Oh, you know,' Dennis said modestly, fixing Colin with a knowing look – one seasoned businessman to another. It was as if I wasn't in the room.

'Take a seat,' Dennis said. There was one armchair directly in front of Dennis's desk and a sofa in the corner. Colin sat in the armchair, and I went towards the sofa. It was a bit far away from the desk, but I'd speak up.

'Don't sit there,' Dennis barked at me. 'The dog sits there.' I peered round the room, but there was no dog. Where the hell was it? Was it some weird test? I was stranded without a seat just in case a dog appeared. I contemplated sitting on the arm of Colin's chair but realised this would make me appear even more ridiculous and not a little gay. Then I saw a chair in the corner behind the door. I wrestled it a little closer to the desk with one hand – trying not to spill my coffee.

Dennis started the meeting without me to avoid

the passable Coco the Clown impression I was doing stage right.

'So, Colin, how can I help?' he said, ominously starting all the way back at once upon a time.

'Have you read the script?' Colin said.

'What's the title?' Dennis wasn't at all embarrassed he didn't know.

'*The Optimist*,' Colin said proudly. I couldn't believe it. He'd got the title wrong. I stared a dagger.

'Sorry. I'm dyslexic,' he said. 'It's called *The Opportunist*.'

There were three script stacks by the side of Dennis's desk. They were all four feet high. He bent over to search and was red faced by the time he found it. I wished I'd been more helpful and written the title on the spine as some of the others had. Fortunately, his search bought me time to position my chair and sit down.

Dennis turned to the last page. They always do. Not to find out whodunit but to see whether it was one hundred and twenty pages long. That's the formula Hollywood likes – a page a minute. Thus, in Hollywood Law, one hundred and twenty pages equate to a two-hour film. Comedies can be a little shorter, because it's hard to keep topping a laugh, and epics a little longer, because epic sets are epically expensive and you might as well show them off for as long as possible. Warren Beatty's script for *Reds*, his film about Russia, apparently ran to four hundred pages. That's either epic or tragic depending on whether you like Warren Beatty's jaw-clenching smile.

'Well, it needs work,' reported Dennis. I thought this a difficult opinion to substantiate as he hadn't read it, but I was probably being over-defensive.

'But they all do,' he added, sweetening the criticism.

'The writer tells me it's in the scam genre. Is that good?' Colin asked, showing off with one of the buzzwords I wished I'd never mentioned. I wondered why Colin was talking about me as if I wasn't in the room. It seemed to be a case of does he take sugar? Yes, I thought. Twice, stirred once to the left.

'Well, who knows what the flavour of the month will be?' Dennis sighed.

'It's a *true* story,' Colin said.

'But does the truth make a good story?' Dennis said.

'There are two good parts. A crooked lawyer and a cab driver,' Colin tried.

'Double the trouble with casting.'

'So, you think you can sell it for me?' Colin said.

'Who to?' Dennis said, sinking into his chair, as

if tired of us already. I wondered when Dennis was going to start answering questions instead of only asking them. Then I wondered why he had a large bowl of sweets on his desk. And finally I wondered when I was going to say something.

'Who to? Why are you asking me?' Colin asked. 'You're the agent.' I was impressed with Colin's directness but worried it might have offended Dennis. He didn't look offended, but he stayed silent. Colin filled the gap. I wished he hadn't.

'You heard of September Films?' I was stunned. Why was he raising a subject that would make us look like failures?

'Yes.'

'They offered me an option.' I didn't like this 'me' talk.

'Congratulations.'

'I told them to fuck off.' I didn't like the 'I' talk either. The profanity I was used to, but Dennis dropped his smile.

'They were only going to give me a quid.'

'Would you buy something before you knew you were going to use it?' Dennis asked.

'Well, if I thought I might use it, I'd pay more than a pound. It's a bloody insult.'

'Well, Colin, if you don't like the way the script acquisition game works, you'll have to produce it yourself.'

'I'm a cab driver, not a bloody producer.' Colin laughed.

'Really? You've got a script without paying for it. Sounds like you're a producer to me.' Dennis turned to smile at me to show he meant no offence. I went to say something, but Colin interrupted. 'I wouldn't know where to start.'

'You've already started,' Dennis assured him. 'All you need now is the rest of the package.'

'*The package?*' Colin said, beating me to it again, but I was happy for him to ask that one in case it was a dumb question.

'Exec producer, director, star. Get those three and you've got your package.'

'Well, no one's stopping you,' Colin tried again.

'I don't do packages. I'm too busy looking after Marlon,' he said with pride.

I was just about to ask what Marlon's favourite ice cream was when, fortunately, the assistant returned and we were bundled out. Colin managed to get a handshake. I didn't. On the way out, the dog returned.

'Good boy,' I said. That's all I said. I'd just attended the most high-powered meeting of my entire career, with one of the most influential players in the business, and I'd only managed to speak to the dog. I wonder whether it was the dog that ate the sweets. I certainly didn't get one.

THE ACCIDENTAL
TOURIST

I wanted to get out of ICM as fast as possible. It was all I could do not to run, but the bloody dog would have come after me. I said nothing in the lift down. I was still fretting about my pathetic performance when we got outside.

'Want a lift home?'

'No, thank you.' I invented some West End errand as my excuse to get away.

'What's the matter?' Colin seemed genuinely concerned.

'I've been dreaming about speaking to a big agent for years and when I get the chance, I blow it.' I didn't like hearing myself whinge.

'You did fine,' he said kindly. 'We got what we need, didn't we?'

'We got nothing.'

'We got a damn good lesson. Now we know about the *package*.'

I couldn't bring myself to acknowledge our new-found advantage. There was a soaring precipice up ahead, and I wasn't sure my climbing boots fitted comfortably. In fact, I didn't even have any climbing boots.

'Who did he say we needed?' Colin asked.

'Exec producer, director, star,' I said, pleased my memory at least made me of some use to our expedition.

'In what order?' Colin asked, more wisely than we realised at the time.

'I don't know.'

'Never mind. They'll get in the cab in the order they will.' Colin smiled. I forced a smile out of politeness. He was trying hard to be chipper. He offered his hand. I shook it.

'Good luck,' I said.

'Fuck luck,' he said. 'We'll make our own.'

It was lucky I kept Colin's taxi free by avoiding his lift because as soon as he'd retrieved his cab from the nearest rank in Rupert Street, the first passenger he picked up just round the corner in Brewer Street was John Frank Rosenblum.

As his supersized name suggests, John Frank is

American. He was also the ultimate Hollywood wannabe. He was my age but already a senior vice president. He was human popcorn: all puffed up and bursting with energy. He never stopped talking. He was always saying 'Gottago'. When Colin met him, he was in London on holiday with his parents, though he probably told his LA colleagues he was 'on location in London, England. Gottago.'

John Frank was treated to a pitch that had by that stage become sophisticated. If Colin's passenger was in the film industry, he took them on a tour of where the scam happened, a version of the research trip he'd taken me on. He pointed out the building he bought for a day and Lawyerland where he met the traitor lawyer and the Savoy where he seduced the diamond broker and the bank where they were nearly caught doing the transfer. Seeing the actual sites lent a lot of credibility to a cab driver, especially as all the while he was admitting to being a con man. When someone actually tells you they're a liar, you don't always believe what they tell you – and you don't always want to do business with them. But John Frank did. He said to Colin, 'Michael will like that.'

'Who's Michael?'

'Michael Phillips.'

'Excuse me,' Colin said, 'but who the fuck is Michael Phillips?'

John Frank smiled at the nerve. 'Have you heard of the movie *Taxi Driver*?'

Colin smiled and waited for more.

'Have you heard of *The Sting*?'

Colin beamed. John Frank smiled; he'd done this before. These two salesmen had a Grandma-and-egg-sucking master class going on between them.

'How about *Close Encounters of the Third Kind*?'

'You're kidding?' Colin said, seeing the first winning symbol spin into place on the slot machine of his future.

'He produced all three.'

'Well, he'll do nicely,' Colin shouted over the PA.

FRANKIE AND JOHNNY

When Colin told me Michael Phillips was getting my script, it didn't take much to imagine a film poster with a strapline saying: FROM THE OSCAR-WINNING PRODUCER OF *TAXI DRIVER* AND *THE STING* COMES A TRUE STORY ABOUT A TAXI DRIVER AND A STING. And written by me would be there as well, probably only in the bottom left-hand corner, but anywhere was fine by me – as long as it wasn't on the back.

I knew who Michael Phillips was. I'd read the famous book by his ex-wife Julia Phillips, *You'll Never Eat Lunch In This Town Again*, the epic Hollywood exposé that predicted the reaction its author would receive after back-stabbing everyone in Tinseltown. Julia and Michael had been Hollywood's hottest producer couple. She was the first woman ever to win a producing Oscar, but that was not enough for her. I say 'was' because, sadly, Julia is dead; she played so hard on a diet of crack cocaine, she now dines alone, hopefully in the restaurant of her choice.

But our excitement eventually waned when we heard nothing. We concluded a big-shot like Michael Phillips was not interested in our little London film. Then, three months later, the phone rang. It was approaching midnight, and I assumed it was Colin with tales of another late-night media pick-up.

'Hello, this is John Frank Rosenblum calling from Lighthouse Productions in Hollywood, California. We'd like to know if the rights to *The Opportunist* are still available,' he said, extremely quickly. I'd never spoken to John Frank, but I soon realised Colin's description of him as a 'Gatling-gob' was accurate. I stalled for a moment. How would Colin have answered? He'd have said they should have phoned earlier; that we were just about to close on a million-dollar deal with someone else, so Lighthouse Productions had better move fast with a better offer.

'Yes, the rights are available,' I said. I wish Colin had taken the call, but my vanity had led me to put my name and phone number on the front cover of the script.

'Everyone in the office loves the script,' he said. 'We just need to get Michael's reaction.'

'Great,' I said. And the call was over. It was my first encounter with Hollywood. At least I'd managed to say more than two words – and to a human being. It was more than I'd managed at ICM. I was getting braver.

I called Colin. 'Did I wake you?' I asked before realising the background noise was traffic. I wondered whether he ever slept.

It seemed strange to be giving him an update. He was usually the one with the news, but it felt good to be contributing to 'the package'.

HIGH SOCIETY

While we waited for Michael Phillips's reaction to the script, Colin continued to trawl the streets of Soho. The numbers are impressive. Everyone who got into Colin's taxi got the pitch. Twenty fares a day, five days a week – one hundred pitches a week. Fifty weeks a year makes five thousand pitches a year. He was relentless because he knew every single passenger might be a good catch. It was like fly-fishing – only Colin was the bait.

Effective though Colin's fishing trips undoubtedly were, the one ingredient they all relied on was a hefty slice of coincidence. He couldn't control who got into his taxi, and if it turned out his passengers weren't in the film business, he couldn't exactly throw them out. But he did try to improve his chances of getting to the right people and making the right impression. In addition to focusing on Soho, where the media crowd work and play, he worked at night, when 'one for the road' might have warmed his captive audience. Alcohol is a useful ingredient when cold-calling cold-hearted Brits.

He refined this tactic by targeting the fashionable and expensive watering holes that attracted the more successful and influential players. Colin's schedule was something like this: the Groucho Club at midnight, Soho House at one and the Met Bar at two. He'd park up outside his target venue with his FOR HIRE light off and then, when what he called 'the right sort' stepped out, he'd turn the FOR HIRE sign back on.

These stalking tactics brought him much success, but it was difficult to find the pieces of the puzzle in the right order. There were plenty of players who were won over far too early. On the music side for example, he sweet-talked Robbie Williams on the way from Berwick Street to Kensington Park Road. Another conquest was Ringo Starr. Colin picked up Ringo and his wife, Barbara Bach, the Bond girl, in Beak Street, and on the way to the Kings Road, the beat behind The Beatles said, 'Count me in, mate.'

The Beatles connection continued when Colin picked up a man who said he was Paul

McCartney's PR. As he liked Colin's story, Colin asked him to ask his boss whether he might be interested in doing the film music.

'He'll be too busy,' the PR guy said.

'Well, ask him anyway,' Colin said.

A week later, coincidence struck again, but on Wardour Street this time, when the same PR guy flagged him again. Colin recognised the PR and said, 'Did you ask him?'

'Ask him yourself,' he said. So Colin did – as soon as Paul McCartney got in.

'I'm too busy,' he said.

He may have said no, but in those early days, Colin got a yes from some other tuneful passengers: Noel Gallagher, Placebo and Björk. Again, before he needed them.

This also happened on the costume side, where he got a yes from John Galliano on the way to Shoreditch and from John Robinson, the head of Jigsaw, travelling from New Bond Street to the Groucho Club. All before he had actors to wear their clothes. Film-making is a circus: you have to keep juggling all the time, but chainsaws can't be kept running forever. When people want you, you may not need them and vice versa. To use up every last big-top metaphor, the lion's either escaped or the clown's not smiling any more.

ANIMAL FARM

I'd given up on John Frank and Lighthouse Productions and was starting to lose faith in Colin's ability to sell the script. Inevitably, Colin was still optimistic because he was still getting rave reactions to his pitch. But we didn't have the package. The plain truth was that we weren't advanced enough; we weren't advancing at all. Certainly, Colin was delighting hundreds of passengers, but you need more than just applause to make a film.

One day, maybe six months later, the phone rang in my study. It was eight in the morning. I was doing sit-ups and was panting like a charity marathon runner in a suit of armour. The sit-ups were required because I'd let time pass since I'd mastered the whippet look and had extended my repertoire of animal impressions to include a less flattering silhouette: an anaconda digesting a watermelon.

I was reluctant to answer the phone because my panting might have sounded suspicious. But if I ignored it and it was my father, he'd have thought I was still in bed. I didn't want him thinking I was an indolent oaf, especially as I was doing sit-ups and, in my book, people who crunch before breakfast deserve a scout badge for will-power, not pinpricks of scorn.

'Hello,' I panted.

'Hello. Can I speak with Colin Hayday, please?'

It was a petrol! He was so polite; he must have waited till after midnight his time to call England in the morning.

'Who's calling?' I asked. Why did I ask that? I was wasting his time. Colin wasn't there and he wasn't going to be there for anyone.

'Michael Phillips,' he answered patiently.

IT WAS MICHAEL PHILLIPS – HIMSELF – FROM HOLLYWOOD, CALIFORNIA.

What a gentle voice he had.

'I'm afraid he's not here. Can I get him to call you back, or maybe take a message?' I grovelled at the feet of the mogul.

There was a pause.

'I'm going away for a few days, so perhaps you'd be so kind as to pass on a message.' He was impossibly polite. What did I expect? With that soft voice, he certainly didn't sound like the straight-talking-hard-hitting-bastard-Hollywood-shark producer I imagined he'd be.

'Fire away,' I said casually, trying to sound helpful.

'Please tell him: I'm sorry but, unfortunately, I can't help him with his movie.'

There was that bloody UNFORTUNATELY again. Only sharks use that word. Just before they start feeding. Yes, I could definitely imagine his dorsal fin breaking the surface. He may have been softly spoken, but I still couldn't believe what he'd just said. I couldn't believe what I was about to say. In fact, I didn't say anything. I shouted. Loudly.

'NOOOOOOOOOOOOOOO.'

Silence.

'I beg your pardon,' he said at last, calmly, clearly confused by my outburst.

'Mr Phillips,' I was bowing low, scrabbling for my manners, 'I'm extremely sorry about that. I was a bit surprised. I'm the writer, you see.'

He said nothing. He wasn't going to help me out. What would Colin have said? He probably would have told the petrol to go torch himself. I had to turn this around. I was on my own. Then I remembered Colin's maxim: if you don't say, you don't get.

'Mr Phillips, can I please ask you to reconsider?'

'I'm sorry, I'm just too busy,' he said, obviously preparing to hang up.

'Michael,' I said more forcefully. 'If I may call you that.' Stop grovelling, I told myself. 'I can't tell you how important it is to have your name on this film – movie.'

He waited.

'This is a story about a taxi driver and a sting, and you produced *Taxi Driver* and *The Sting*.' I surprised myself – I thought I was sounding like a rather good salesman.

'I know what I produced,' he said wearily. He thought I was the most annoying salesman in the world.

I took another breath and tried again: 'It's the classic underdog tale of the little guy who learns how to twist the system. He takes on everyone and wins, but even when he makes it, he's betrayed by the one person who's closest to him.'

Silence.

I knew it wasn't going well. He was still hungry for more. I was pleased I wasn't with him in person. I'd have been staring at his shark's teeth at that point – maybe even his tonsils.

I needed a different angle. Then I remembered the oldest trick in the book: flattery – and lots of it. I needed Oscar acceptance speech flattery.

'Michael, we *love* your work. *Everyone* loves your work. If you stop ten people in the street, any ten people, and ask them what their favourite movie is, five will say *Taxi Driver* and the other five *The Sting*. Every time. With you at the helm, we'll score ten out of ten. We can't lose,' I ranted – and panted.

Then I noticed how noisy I sounded and held my breath.

The silence was unbearable. So was the lack of oxygen.

Then, I thought I heard him smile. What made me smile was hearing him say: 'I'll call you back.'

We still had a chance. His no wasn't a NO. Yet. I'd shouted at him and he hadn't shouted back. I thought about calling Colin to get his advice – or maybe I could have passed the buck. He'd deal with this much better than me. He was used to haggling. He knew about high-powered deals. He knew the rules of poker. But I couldn't call. If Michael called back and I was blocking the line, he'd get the answer machine and leave the 'No' message he'd planned to. It was the longest wait of my amateur little life.

Five minutes later, the phone rang. I had to stop myself picking it up straight away. I didn't want to seem desperate. I wanted my hello to sound nonchalant, but, instead, I sounded ridiculous: breathy, like a stoned John Wayne.

'Heeellloooo.' Or maybe I didn't even sound like a man. I hoped I didn't sound like Audrey Hepburn.

'You can use my name as executive producer,' Michael said, without saying hello. 'I want two point five per cent of the gross budget as my fee and the same percentage of the net profit. I think you'll find that's fair. My lawyer will send you the contract. Now I want to make it clear. I'm not offering to be a producer. You're doing the work, not me. If my name helps, that's fine.'

'Thank you, Michael, thank you.'

'Don't thank me, because I'm not doing anything. But I will wish you luck,' he said. 'You're gonna need it. Putting together a movie – it's damn hard. The best way I can describe it – it's like trying to catch lightning – in a bottle.'

BEOWULF

'THANK *YOU*,' shouted Colin, slapping my bony left shoulder. He'd rushed over so fast, the pterodactyl screech of the cab's brakes was still echoing round the block.

'I thought you'd be pissed off I didn't haggle a better deal,' I said. 'We've got to catch the lightning on our own.'

'It's a brilliant deal. We've got *his name*. We've got the first piece of the package. We've got kosher,' he yelled. I liked that line. We'd got kosher. In truth, we'd got lucky. We'd had no idea how to put together a package, but we'd unwittingly started by doing it in the right order.

If you're a nobody, you need credibility and the fastest way to get it is to borrow a famous name. Essentially, that's all an executive producer is, but you need it as the first piece of your package. It's the only way to open doors. Getting an executive producer is common practice. You've probably seen Spielberg's name as executive producer on a lot of films. That's because he's got 'cred' and he can earn without having to do anything. That's not a criticism. He's worked hard. Let him enjoy his reputation.

Even second-hand fame will do. Guy Ritchie, Mr Madonna, got Trudie Styler, Mrs Sting, to lend her shoulder to *Lock, Stock and Two Smoking Barrels*. It probably didn't hurt that the Madonnas and the Stings are neighbours in Wiltshire or that Guy's producer's father is Robert Vaughan, the Man From Uncle. That's a lot of apostrophes and a lot of confused relations, but they're all famous or half famous and they all could be executive producers.

Colin was driving around Soho, bragging that our executive producer was an Oscar winner, when he got to the corner of Great Marlborough Street and Poland Street. Graham Baker got in. He's a film director. Now, here's another packaging lesson. You'll remember there were three elements to the package: executive producer, director, star. You go for the actors last. In other words, after you've got a director. The reason's simple: actors want to know who's going to direct them. Actors rarely commit to a project if they don't know who's going to tell them what to do. Actors are insecure that way. Actors are insecure full stop. I'm not being rude. Ask them. They'll tell you – over and over again.

Colin started on Graham with one of his most effective lines.

'Are you in advertising?'

'No, I'm in films,' Graham corrected him.

Colin's advertising line was a good one. It always flushed out the film crowd. Only people in advertising want to be in advertising, until they want to get out. And most of them want to get into films. Most advert directors, or commercials directors as they title themselves, want to direct films, but few succeed. Alan Parker and Ridley Scott are famous success stories, but they are exceptions. Commercials directors generally don't have a good reputation for directing people. They can make a loaf of bread look fantastic – even edible – but give them an actor and they'll make them look – stale. This explains why Graham was keen to pin his tail on the cinema stallion rather than the commercial donkey.

Graham told Colin he'd directed *Alien Nation*, the sci-fi classic starring James Caan.

'I've heard of him,' Colin said, enjoying being the movie buff.

Graham told Colin he'd directed *The Final Conflict* with Sam Neill, the third film in the *Omen* trilogy. At the time, Graham was working with Christopher Lambert on an adaptation of the epic medieval poem *Beowulf*.

In return, Colin told Graham about his scam and Graham liked it.

'I like it,' he said.

'Speak to my executive producer,' Colin said, boasting.

Graham humoured him. 'Who's your executive producer?'

'Michael Phillips.'

Graham was stunned. 'Michael Phillips? Where did you find him?'

'The same place I found you. In the back of a cab.'

'I nearly made a film with him last year,' Graham said.

'You'll do,' Colin said.

'What?' Graham was understandably perplexed.

'Give Michael a call and tell him I've just met our director.'

Colin had done it again. We had the second piece of the package. One to go: the star.

EVITA

Colin was in Wardour Street when he picked up Sarah Crowe, a truly wonderful casting director who was to become the project's most tireless and loyal supporter. His timing in meeting Sarah was lucky because her career was just starting to blossom. She'd been working on the casting for *Absolutely Fabulous*, and *Ab Fab* became a huge hit.

Riding this wave allowed Sarah to set up her own agency, and she has since become absolutely fabulously successful in her own right, working with lots of stars and casting many popular TV shows and films. If we'd met her now, she'd be far too busy to see us, but back then she kindly agreed to look at the script. She read it overnight, which in itself is a huge favour, and she liked it and offered to get it to some actors.

She taught us a lot. For a start, she taught us that casting is much more complicated than we'd expected. Everyone thinks casting is easy. They think it's simply a matter of picking your favourite actors, just like in some pub game where everyone chips in with their ideal cast for a remake of something like *The A Team* or *The Six Million Dollar Man*. In reality, casting is a meticulous, almost scientific, process of elimination.

Sarah was highly methodical. First off, she focused our minds on Colin's age. When writing the script, I'd envisaged Colin as Michael Caine. Unfortunately, the picture I had in my head was of a cocksure Alfie in 1966, when Caine was in his early thirties. Our discussions with Sarah were happening thirty years later. Sadly, my hero Caine, although still cocksure no doubt, was a little too old.

We told Sarah we'd approached another genuine geezer, Bob Hoskins, and she asked why we'd picked someone who was fifty. We didn't know. Oh yes, it was because Colin could get to his PA. Sarah smiled. As our answer made us look more than a bit amateur, I overcompensated by announcing purposefully that a thirty-something actor should play Colin to give the character maximum audience appeal. I had no idea what I was talking about, but Colin agreed with me.

Amazingly, so did Sarah. But she had a sound professional reason. She explained that although Colin had been fifty in reality, it was a difficult age for many distributors' target audience – namely teenagers. The logic was straightforward: teenagers don't go to the cinema to see their dads. At last we had a proper reason for setting Colin at the safer age of thirty-something. And we didn't have to be upset that Bob Hoskins had turned us down. And, on top of that, Sarah suggested we could cast the lawyer the same age and thus the film would be a classic buddy movie.

Having chosen Colin's age, Sarah focused on the route that would help us raise finance. This generally means choosing a bankable star, which generally means choosing an American. But we all hated the idea of an American having a go at a cockney accent for three simple reasons: Dick Van Dyke.

Our paranoia over accents thus ruled out some great actors on the simple grounds of geography. Ewan McGregor and Robert Carlyle were too Scottish. Liam Neeson, Pierce Brosnan and Gabriel Byrne were too Irish. And Sean Bean was too northern. We'd hit the bottom of the barrel.

In session after session, increasingly desperate ideas flew in from nowhere but were soon shot down. Gary Oldman is a brilliant actor, but I decided he came across as a psychopath. And Ray Winstone, Johnny Lee Miller and Sean Pertwee weren't big enough names. (This was the mid-'90s and Colin and I hadn't heard of Jude Law.) Our list of hot thirty-something British actors was eventually whittled down to Daniel Day Lewis, Hugh Grant, Colin Firth and Ralph Fiennes. We clearly had a problem. They can all act – but they're toffs.

At least we wouldn't have a problem casting our toff lawyer, given we'd already agreed not to make him Burmese (on the assumption that Burmese actors aren't an international draw). But ours was a film about a cab driver first and foremost, not a lawyer. We still needed our streetwise, street-tough hero.

Then Sarah hit gold. She remembered Tim Roth. How could we have forgotten? He was hot. A hot dog, no less. Indeed, a Reservoir Dog.

SHERLOCK HOLMES

Graham Baker had an elegant apartment in a grand Art Deco block just off Baker Street. His estate agent was probably very smug about the naming coincidence. It was just round the corner from where Sherlock Holmes was supposed to have lived. We met Graham one afternoon to investigate our casting riddle. Sarah came with us to help persuade Graham that Tim Roth was our man. She told us we should respect the courtesy that the director traditionally has final say in casting the lead. We were all nervous because Tim Roth was not a huge star, but we had to persuade Graham that he was perfect for us. We had to succeed because we didn't have any other suggestions.

Graham is a jazz fan and had a grand piano in

the sitting room, which I'm sure delighted his neighbours. The meeting started in a laid-back sort of way with Graham tinkling his ivories. He was in charge and we knew it. His experience as a film-maker dwarfed ours. Indeed, we had no experience at all, but Graham was welcoming and he kindly avoided treating us like novices. He'd had a long chat with Michael Phillips the night before. Whatever had been said was enough to persuade Graham to come on board.

As the meeting was going well, Colin threw in Sarah's brilliant idea about Tim Roth. This deflated Graham so much he stopped playing the piano and closed the lid with alarming finality.

'He's too indie,' Graham declared. Graham looked round the room, waiting for more. We knew he wanted a bigger name, but we had no one else to offer. We stayed silent.

'How about Hugh Grant?' Graham said.

'For the cabbie?' I gulped, incredulous.

'Absolutely,' Graham said.

'He's a toff,' I said. I laughed mockingly, but I was on my own. I let my laugh peter out. Awkward silence.

'What do you think, Col?' Graham said.

'Whatever it takes,' Colin said. Graham took this as agreement and resumed playing the piano.

I thought Hugh Grant was completely wrong. I

stared a rebuke at Colin, but he simply shrugged his shoulders. Then I glanced at Sarah, who looked slightly pained, but in the absence of an alternative she stayed diplomatically quiet.

Graham beamed. 'Yes, I think it could be quite interesting.'

'He's not street enough,' I said. I really didn't like the way it was going. I was being as ignored as I'd heard all screenwriters are.

But I knew I was right. Hugh Grant was the wrong choice to play Colin. He was charming and good looking and popular for sure, but he was too damn predictable.

That night, Hugh Grant was arrested in the streets of Los Angeles with a prostitute optimistically christened Divine Brown.

THE RIGHT STUFF

When I saw Hugh Grant on the news, I was impressed. I didn't think he had it in him. I still thought he'd be wrong as a cab-driving con man, but I had to concede he had far more range than I'd given him credit for. In fact, I feared his new-found street cred would convince Graham even more. I was resigning myself to defeat when I heard from Sarah that Graham had lost interest in Hugh Grant. As he disapproved of the negative publicity that was already spreading, he'd reconsidered Tim Roth and dubbed him the right man. Great. We were back up to speed and, more importantly, we were all in agreement.

Sarah sent the script to Tim Roth's agent, Stephanie Randall, who raved about it. Unfortunately, she also said, 'Is finance in place?'

Of course, Sarah had to say no. She phoned Colin and said, 'We need finance.'

'Can't we get him to say yes first and then get the money?' Colin asked.

'Stephanie doesn't work that way,' Sarah said. 'If she said yes to us, she'd be tying him up and might have to turn down another film that was already funded. It's understandable, Colin. Would you sell your car to someone who only might have the money?'

'Don't worry. I'll call Michael,' Colin said calmly. Surely he'd tell us what we had to do to get the last piece of the package.

That night, in the small hours because of the time difference, Colin phoned Lighthouse Productions and asked for Michael, but, as he was away, he was put through to Gatling-gob John Frank.

'Hello, this is John Frank Rosenblum from Lighthouse Productions,' he said, as quickly as ever.

'I know. I called you,' said Colin, with no hello.

John Frank recognised Colin's accent. 'Oh. Hi, Colin.'

'Where's Michael?'

'He's away at a yoga retreat.'

'Maybe you can tell me. How do we get the money to pay for Tim Roth? Do we go to Warner Brothers or something?'

'I don't think we should go to the studios yet,' John Frank said. Colin ignored the 'we'. He'd never seen John Frank as the main man, but he was getting interested in what he had to say.

John Frank explained we should avoid the studios because they'd take over the project and cut us out.

'Frankly, they'd get in one of their writers,' he said. As Colin knew that would upset me, he agreed it was right to avoid the studios.

'Plus, if our timing's out, we might get put into turnaround,' he told Colin.

'What's turnaround?'

'If the studio head changes, and they do every couple of years, you're dealing with another Hollywood ego, so your film turns around. Your green light turns back to red because the new boss will never finish their predecessor's projects. Why would they? If the project bombs, it's their fault. If it succeeds, they have to share the glory.'

Colin was already convinced we shouldn't go to the studios when John Frank added a final lesson to show he knew how the Hollywood game works.

'As a halfway house, we could go to a star with an output deal.'

'What's an output deal?'

'It's an arrangement where the studio gets first refusal on a star's personal output. They usually set up a star with an office on their lot, like those cute bungalows in *The Player*. The studio pays for the office and in return they get first refusal on the personal projects the star is developing for himself or herself to star in.'

'I don't get it. Are you saying we *are* going to the studios now?' Colin said, confused.

'No. Because none of your British actors have output deals and you guys don't want a Yank driving your cab.'

'So if we don't go to the studios, who do we go to?' Colin said.

'We'll go independent,' said John Frank, chirpily, clearly delighted to be playing the general.

'I'll put what we've got to a few independent distributors I know and see what they'll pay for Tim Roth,' speed-talked John Frank. 'But if you guys want me to represent you, I'll need your authority. You'll have to make me a producer. You think about it. Gottago.'

Colin told me later he hadn't dissuaded John Frank from taking charge of the Hollywood end. He felt it was fine if John Frank muscled in on the project, as Michael was never going to do anything.

'I don't want to split the pie any more, but what choice have we got?' Colin said.

'Without a star, we don't have a pie. We need John Frank,' I said.

'Well, he talks so bloody fast, at least it'll keep the phone bills down,' Colin said.

That was the next lesson. We had to get our package to the distributors. This is how it was going to work: the distributor would provide the cash to make the film and in return they would be the first to get their money back from the box office ticket sales plus they would take at least forty per cent of any profits. That's a massively high interest rate for a loan. Regular banks charge less than ten per cent interest on a loan. Even rip-off credit cards charge less than thirty per cent. But a regular bank would never lend several million dollars for a highly speculative venture with no security. And what security did we have? Colin's cab? No, it was rented. We had to go to distributors because they were the only people who might be insane enough to risk millions of dollars on nothing more than a clutch of Colin's passengers and my typing.

THE MADNESS OF KING GEORGE

Because John Frank was just the little guy using his boss's name, we guessed it would take him a long time to raise the offer money for Tim Roth. We were worried our fragile package might break apart in the meantime if we didn't maintain the momentum. Sarah came up with an ingenious plan. She would try to make the project more attractive to Tim Roth by going for the supporting cast at the same time. She was hoping to fill the shoes of the other key players: the lawyer's boss and the diamond broker and the hit men. The idea was that the supporting cast would be easier to attract because asking an actor for a couple of days' work was less demanding than asking a lead to give up six months for a film that wasn't even funded. Then, if she got the supporting cast to commit in principle, Tim Roth might see the project as more complete. It was a clever plan but highly risky because, as Colin had discovered, the British film industry is a small community centred in a gossipy Soho, and if word got round that the supporting actors had said no, Tim Roth would hear about it and be put off for good.

Colin and I had become so used to waiting months for decisions, we weren't expecting Sarah to have an answer within a week. She phoned and coolly mentioned that Nigel Hawthorne might be interested in playing Smedley, the lawyer's boss. We were stunned: we'd got our first actor.

SALEM'S LOT

Nigel Hawthorne's interest started a run of good luck. A week later, Colin phoned to say he'd picked up David Soul's girlfriend. She thought he might be interested in playing one of the hitmen. He liked bad-guy parts, apparently. That was fine by me. I'd been a huge fan of *Starsky and Hutch* as a kid. I could see him driving a silver Jag – even though he might have preferred a red one with a white stripe down the side.

BEN HUR

A couple of weeks after that, Sarah phoned to say Helen Mirren might be interested in playing the diamond broker. I hoped she'd been flattered I'd written the part specifically for her.

THE THREE MUSKETEERS

A couple of weeks after that, Sarah phoned to say Michael York might be interested in playing the lawyer's boss. Of course, we already had a Smedley, but my mother liked Michael York. Everyone's mother liked the idea of swashbuckling with D'Artagnan.

UNDER MILK WOOD

A couple of weeks after that, Sarah phoned to say Catherine Zeta Jones might be interested in playing the diamond broker. This was before she married Michael Douglas. She's now a diamond broker in her own right.

We were suddenly being blinded by choice. But we still had no money to pay for anyone. Even Colin was starting to get nervous. He called John Frank and demanded an update from the independents. John Frank said, 'I absolutely, totally, one hundred per cent guarantee to call you back in one week.'

MUSIC OF CHANCE

Two weeks later, John Frank phoned to say he was still waiting on the independents, but he did have some good news: Stewart Copeland might be interested in doing the soundtrack. Stewart is the ex-drummer and founder of The Police. His soundtracks are, not surprisingly, extremely percussive. I particularly liked the score he wrote for *Rumble Fish*, Coppola's stylised buddy movie starring Matt Dillon and Mickey Rourke.

Nonetheless, music wasn't our problem. Not forgetting Ringo Starr, we had two drummers offering to do the soundtrack. In addition to the drummers, Colin could return to the encounters that have already been mentioned (Robbie Williams, Oasis, Placebo and Björk) plus the acts he'd subsequently chatted up: Simple Minds, The

Charlatans, Iron Maiden and William Orbit. What we needed was some money to pay for our actors. Then we could really make some music.

THE HANDMAID'S TALE

A week later, John Frank phoned to say the editor who'd hand-spliced *The Godfather* might be interested in cutting the film. John Frank was pleased with himself. Colin wasn't. He said, 'Fuck the editing. Even I know that comes at the end. What about the money for Tim Roth?' Then Colin paraphrased Jerry Maguire, shouting, 'Show me the fucking money.'

SPARTACUS

We were beyond desperate. We'd all but hired half of Soho and didn't have a penny to pay for anyone. Poor Sarah was getting calls from every actor's agent in London; they were demanding to know whether we were making a film or not.

Finally, a month later, John Frank called Colin and said, 'I've got a bite.'

'Who from?'

'CineCentury.'

'Who?' Colin said.

'They're independent distributors,' John Frank said.

'Yeah. They're so bloody independent, I've never heard of them.'

'They're happy with a fifteen-million budget.'

That shut him up.

'We're flying over tomorrow,' John Frank said. 'Let's meet.'

Colin came round to my flat to deliver the good news in person.

'What are we going to ask them for?' I asked.

'Whatever we can get.'

'What about the credits?'

'Well, producer would be nice,' he said.

'They'll want to bring in someone who's actually made a film,' I said. 'They'll get the producer credit.'

'All right, then, but definitely co-producer. And the same for you,' he said.

'Written by is fine for me.'

He shook his head emphatically. 'No. I told you fifty-fifty. If I get co-producer, so do you.'

'But you did all the work,' I said. 'You put the package together. I just did the typing.'

'What do you mean? It was your idea to network Soho. You got Michael Phillips. No, we did it together.'

That felt good. At last, we really were partners.

BREAKFAST AT TIFFANY'S

We met at the Ritz Hotel for a 'power breakfast powwow', as John Frank put it. I thought it was a touristy choice, but if they were staying five-star, we knew we were dealing with players.

We arrived early, at just after eight. Colin had picked me up in the taxi on his way over and ten minutes later we were in the foyer, having dumped the taxi in a nearby rank.

We were sitting on a sofa, admiring the sweeping staircase while we waited for our new colleagues. We'd got there early because we were meeting Michael and the head of CineCentury, both for the first time. I was excited. The lift pinged open and John Frank bowled out wearing jeans and a hairstyle that can only be described as Billy Ray Cyrus. If you're not a fan of country and western music, imagine a brunette Michael Bolton, receding on top and mullet at back. It was the first time I'd met John Frank. As I was trying to look media smart, I was wearing all black. I'd only recently stepped from the shower and my hair was still damp and slicked – I looked like a plastic gangster. John Frank looked like a banjo player from the woods. Colin wore a suit as usual and was the only one of us who could have avoided being cast in a pantomime.

'Where's Michael?' Colin said immediately, before the hellos had melted.

'What?' John Frank said, confused.

'He's not fucking coming, is he?' Colin snapped.

John Frank put his hands up defensively, like a mime artist. 'Hold up there, Colin. I never said Michael was coming. But it's OK, he told me what to say.'

'I'm getting a bit bloody tired of hearing about Michael without ever meeting him. We're trying to cut a deal here. Where is he?'

'He's got really into his yoga. He has a class today.'

'Who with? The Dalai Lama?' Colin said without smiling.

John Frank stayed silent. Like me, he was surprised by Colin's hostility. But rather than back down, Colin continued the attack.

'So who are we meeting from CineCentury? The man or the boy?'

I found Colin's rudeness embarrassing. So did John Frank.

'His wife, actually,' John Frank said, shifting his weight like he needed the bathroom.

'What?' said Colin, almost spitting.

'We're meeting his wife, but she doesn't like people to know she's his wife.'

Colin leaned over John Frank and whispered mischievously, 'Well, why did you tell me?'

John Frank looked like he was going to cross his legs. He was grateful for the distraction when the revolving door spun a blonde into the foyer. It was the wife. Her grown-up trouser suit did little to hide her youth; she looked to be in her twenties. We'll call her Tiffany because it's become a popular British name and she was British. I was disappointed. If we were selling our film to Hollywood, the least they could have done was send a petrol.

'Hi there,' she said in an Estuary accent that had gone west but occasionally forgot its passport. Sometimes she sounded Braintree, Essex, and sometimes brainless, LA.

'I'm Tiffany. I'm senior vice-president of acquisitions at CineCentury.'

'Really?' Colin said. 'I'm Colin.' Now the amateur dramatics had started, he flicked off the house lights and sprang into one of his charm offensives. He took her hand more smoothly than Valentino. 'What a lovely long title you have.'

Despite Colin's frustration, John Frank had been working hard for us and was a considerable way into a complicated deal. For those not familiar with international film distribution, the rights to a film tend to be split into territories. As the Americans invented the business, they named it from their point of view. Rights in America are therefore called 'Domestic' and rights in the rest of the world are known as 'International' or 'Foreign'. These International rights can then be split further into other territories such as Europe and the Far East.

CineCentury dealt in International rights, hence the logic of their British connection. Because of the shared language, to American distributors Britain is one of the more important territories within the International pot. John Frank's plan was to raise half the budget by selling International to CineCentury. He hoped to get the other half by selling Domestic (American rights) to Miramax. He'd been courting them for weeks. Miramax were impressed by the package, not least because they knew Michael Phillips well. But Miramax didn't get their wily reputation from nowhere and they certainly showed that they'd earned it in our case. They insisted that because our film was about a British subject it should open in the UK first. They refused to commit to the American rights until at least the UK part of the International rights had been sold. They wanted to be sure our London film had the backing of London money. Having the famous Miramax looking at American rights might be considered an impressive result, but without selling at least the UK part of the International rights first, we had nothing. This meant we needed CineCentury. We needed Tiffany. But more than anything we needed Colin to keep being nice to Tiffany.

As we settled down round the breakfast table, Colin was the first to speak.

'So, Tiffany, what do we need to do to make you happy?'

HELLRAISER

The meeting with Hollywood was going surprisingly well. Tiffany and John Frank were trying to outbid each other with compliments about the script. It was flattering to think everyone was there because of what I'd written. Of course, they weren't. I failed to realise at first that no one had read the latest draft. Except Colin, which is saying something of someone with severe dyslexia. The rest gave themselves away because, once diplomacy had ensured the compliments were safely on record, suggestions of wholesale changes started flying across the table, all escorted with a Hollywood smile.

It always amazes me what liberties people feel they can take with someone else's script. Every other creative process is automatically accorded more respect. If an artist unveiled their latest portrait, no one would pick up a brush and daub a moustache on it. Scripts, on the other hand, are covered with everyone else's facial hair.

'I think Colin should get the girl,' John Frank suggested. 'At the end, they should be riding off into the sunset.' How cheesy was that? He just wanted to look like a romantic in front of Tiffany. I leapt to my own defence.

'The key relationship is between the cab driver and the bent lawyer,' I said.

'Is this a gay movie?' John Frank said, shocked.

'No,' I said huffily. 'It's just that I don't think we should be distracted by the diamond broker.'

'Gay could be interesting,' Tiffany said.

'No it wouldn't,' Colin said. I threw him a don't-answer-back stare.

'If we make the diamond broker a bigger part, we could go for a bigger name,' Tiffany said.

'And a happy ending,' John Frank threw in.

'What?' I was whimpering.

'The cab driver's got to get the diamonds,' John Frank said.

Colin suddenly leant forward and interrupted. 'Look. Let's leave his script alone for a minute. It's good enough to get you all here, so let's talk about International rights.'

Everyone was staring at Colin. I was grateful for

the defence of my script but not that the atmosphere had become hostile again.

'Tiffany, what do you want?' Colin said.

Tiffany composed a demure smile. 'Peter, that's the CEO of CineCentury . . .' I looked at Colin and hoped he'd stay silent. He did. Tiffany continued. 'If we're going to take on International rights, Peter wants me to be credited as a producer – single frame, first show, same font size as you guys.'

Colin looked amazed. 'I've had to package this thing to earn my credit,' he said. 'Even John Frank has worked his balls off. What exactly have you done?'

I was surprised Colin had praised John Frank. But a bowline knot was forming in my bowels. Tiffany stayed impressively calm. 'I think it's reasonable for Peter to have someone supervise the spending of his money.'

It was a fair answer. Colin's reply was anything but.

'Can you drive? Because maybe you can play the cab driver as well.'

Bloody hell, the gloves were off. I waited for Tiffany's response. She stood up. I thought she was going to slap him.

'If you'll excuse me. I need the bathroom.' And she disappeared.

The pause brought no relief.

'What does she mean, *bathroom*?' Colin scoffed. 'Bathroom? She ain't even a petrol.'

When she was clearly out of earshot, I turned to Colin. I was furious. Just when I'd started to think he was a decent partner, the aggression I'd feared from the start had surfaced to become a liability – and at the worst possible time.

'What are you doing?' I said hissing. 'Can you hear yourself? *She's – the – money.* She's all we've got. Show some respect, will you? Please!'

When Tiffany returned from powdering her nose, she was all smiles again, but it was a thin veil. I decided to take charge, to keep Colin at bay.

'I'm sure that'll be fine,' I said. 'We don't need to fall out over a credit. So what happens next?'

'Get yourself a star and you've got a deal,' she said.

Colin looked furious.

'Look,' he said, leaning forward again to make a point without shouting. 'We've got Helen Mirren, Nigel Hawthorne, David Soul, Catherine Zeta Jones, Michael York . . . Who else do you want? Godzilla?'

'But you haven't got the lead,' she said forcefully.

'Give us some money and we'll get Tim Roth,' Colin said. It was almost a demand.

'No,' she said.

'Why not?' Colin said.

'I don't like Tim Roth.'

'What do you mean?' said Colin mockingly. 'Everyone likes Tim Roth. Michael likes Tim Roth. Graham likes Tim Roth. I like Tim Roth . . .'

'I don't think he can carry this film,' she interrupted.

Hideous silence.

'We can boost him a bit. We'll get a name to be the lawyer,' I tried.

'What about Hugh Grant?' Colin said in desperation.

I stared wildly at him.

'As the lawyer,' he added.

'This is a film about a cab driver,' Tiffany said haughtily. 'The cab driver has to be the star.' And we knew she was right.

'What about if we launch a star – with an unknown as the cabbie – and surround him with the stars we've got?' I said.

'Peter won't risk his money on an unknown.'

'Well, darlin, who the hell will your husband pay for?' Colin smiled cheekily, looking round the table for support.

It was probably the 'darlin' that did it.

'You're the producers. Find us a star – not Tim Roth – and we'll buy International. I can't say it any plainer than that.'

And she was gone.

CATCH-22

I couldn't believe how disappointed I felt after the meeting with CineCentury. It reminded me of a childhood nightmare: I'd woken on Christmas morning, but I couldn't wake anyone and the presents were round the tree, but I couldn't find my glasses and I couldn't read the tags and I didn't know which gifts were for me and I just had to sit there opening nothing.

I was angry CineCentury were being so unhelpful. Tiffany hadn't been plain at all. If only she'd told us who they would finance, we'd get them. I was also angry we couldn't think of anyone more bankable than Tim Roth. And why weren't they prepared to take a risk on an unknown surrounded by stars? It was a common strategy.

I was livid about how rude Colin had been to Tiffany and John Frank. But John Frank had thicker skin than mine. He left for LA promising to take the package to the big studios because we weren't getting anywhere with the independents. But our parting conversation didn't exactly fill me with the confidence that our team was still in love.

'You should've done it anyway,' Colin said.

'Come on, Colin,' I said, coming to John Frank's defence. 'We all agreed not to go to the studios first.'

'You didn't want them to take over your project,' John Frank reminded Colin. 'They would have cut you out.'

'They would've cut *you* out, you mean,' Colin said harshly.

'Gottago,' John Frank said.

A week later, I woke up to find an answer machine message from John Frank. He'd called in the middle of the night. Either he'd forgotten the time difference or he was deliberately avoiding a conversation. I think he called me because he was afraid of Colin, who always gave him a hard time. By that I mean Colin asked him sensible questions about raising production money whereas I just asked after Hollywood stars such as Paul Newman and Robert DeNiro. John Frank's answer was always, 'I haven't met them, but they're good friends of Michael's.'

The message went: 'Hi – this is John Frank – today I submitted to Fox and Universal – tomorrow Paramount and Sony – I also sent it to a couple of producers who have studio deals – Don Murphy with Disney – he did *Mortal Kombat* – and Tom Desanto with Fox – he did *Usual Suspects* – I'll let you know – Gottago.'

I had to play it back three times to write down all the names. I read them over the phone to Colin.

'I'm impressed,' Colin said – for the first time.

ALL QUIET ON THE WESTERN FRONT

Colin and I were delighted Fox and Universal and Paramount were looking at our package, even though we might have to give up control. We dreamed of a bidding war that would see our names plastered all over the *Hollywood Reporter*. The truth is, anyone in the film business doesn't feel they're really in the film business until they're dealing with the studios.

Colin was so excited he called John Frank the next day. He tried him at Lighthouse Productions' office but a receptionist said he was 'on a special assignment'. As Colin couldn't wait, he tried him at home. But all he got was his answer machine – for two months. All answer machine messages are annoying, but John Frank's was nails-on-ablackboard unbearable. It was a soundbite from some '50s movie about Hollywood. An eager producer was saying in a squeaky voice not dissimilar to John Frank's, 'You mean to say, if we stick to petty cash we could bring this picture in for under twenty grand?'

It was as annoying as this:

'You mean to say, if we stick to petty cash we could bring this picture in for under twenty grand?'

'You mean to say, if we stick to petty cash we could bring this picture in for under twenty grand?'

'You mean to say, if we stick to petty cash we could bring this picture in for under twenty grand?'

'You mean to say, if we stick to petty cash we could bring this picture in for under twenty grand?'

'You mean to say, if we stick to petty cash we could bring this picture in for under twenty grand?'

'You mean to say, if we stick to petty cash we could bring this picture in for under twenty grand?'

'You mean to say, if we stick to petty cash we could bring this picture in for under twenty grand?'

'You mean to say, if we stick to petty cash we could bring this picture in for under twenty grand?'

'You mean to say, if we stick to petty cash we could bring this picture in for under twenty grand?'

'You mean to say, if we stick to petty cash we could bring this picture in for under twenty grand?'

'You mean to say, if we stick to petty cash we could bring this picture in for under twenty grand?'

'You mean to say, if we stick to petty cash we could bring this picture in for under twenty grand?'

'You mean to say, if we stick to petty cash we could bring this picture in for under twenty grand?'

'You mean to say, if we stick to petty cash we could bring this picture in for under twenty grand?'

See what I mean?

PSYCHO

Colin ditched his manners. Previously, he'd called John Frank at night, daytime for John Frank. But if John Frank was refusing to return his calls, Colin would refuse to let John Frank sleep. He called him at three in the morning. A sleepy voice answered.

'Where the fuck have you been?' Colin shouted.

Of course John Frank knew it was Colin.

'I've been on holiday,' John Frank said.

'Well, now you're back, what's been happening?'

'CineCentury are still interested, if we get a star.'

'Tell me something I don't know.'

'Well, Miramax are still in the frame, but we've got to sell Foreign first.'

'Jesus!' Colin screamed. 'Have I waited two months to hear the same record?'

'Colin, you've got to be patient. I'm trying to raise millions of dollars here. This is a very delicate business. Look, Colin, I gottago.'

Colin burst in before he could go.

'I've tried being patient and I don't need it. John Frank, you're a waste of space. So all I've got left to say is – you gottago fuck yourself.'

And he slammed down the phone.

PRIDE AND PREJUDICE

Colin sounded unusually subdued over the phone.

'I've just spoken to John Frank.'

I was delighted by any news at all. 'What did he say?'

'Nothing.'

'What do you mean?'

'Nothing's fucking happened.' The swearing seemed a little inappropriate.

'What do you mean?'

'Everything's still the same.'

'I guess we'll just have to be patient,' I said.

'Not with him, we won't.'

I suddenly saw a penny.

'What do you mean?'

'He's not right for us.'

The penny dropped.

'No, Colin.'

'He was fucking useless.' Colin was reassuring himself.

'What do you mean "was"? Did he quit?'

Colin refused to answer. I couldn't believe what this could mean. I couldn't believe I didn't raise my voice.

'Don't tell me you fired him, Colin.'

No answer.

Finally, 'We're better off without him.'

HE HAD FIRED HIM.

'You think we're better off now, do you?' I said.

'Too fucking right.'

'What do you reckon *I* think about it?' I asked quietly.

Colin didn't answer.

Then I raised my voice.

'You don't know what I think, do you?'

I waited, my silence demanding an answer.

'No,' he conceded.

'You don't know because you didn't ask.'

Silence.

'Again!' I added.

Colin hid in silence. That made me even more furious.

'What did I tell you last time?'

No answer.

'What was it you told me? Fifty-fifty?' I said, mocking.

'He's done *nothing*,' Colin said.

'Well, you've done something, haven't you? You've completely fucked our chances. We're back to square one. The only thing holding this film together was the vague promise that an Oscar-winning producer was holding it together. And now who's in charge? A nobody writer and a nobody con man.'

Colin was shocked by my outburst. I'd surprised myself, but the depth of my loathing was unfathomable.

'Frankly, Colin,' I concluded, 'if I'm going to be a nobody, I'll do it on my own.'

'What do you mean?' Colin demanded.

'You're on your own.'

'But we're partners,' Colin said resolutely.

'Not any more. I resign.' And I hung up. Or more accurately, I slammed the phone down.

The lightning had gone.

As far as I was concerned, it was bloody well over.

THE END

AND THEN THERE WERE NONE

I'd given up. I knew it and hated being a quitter, but it seemed the only decision. There was the principle of the thing. Yet again, he'd ignored our partnership. And film-making is a partnership. He clearly was wrong for me. He'd killed the project. I'd take what I'd learned and write another script – based on reality, of course. I'd learned that lesson. And I'd package it myself. I'd been to a few meetings. I knew what to say. It would be fine.

Then the phone rang. I let the answer machine take it in case it was Colin. It was Colin.

'I need to talk to you.' His voice didn't sound apologetic, but I didn't expect it to. Colin is clearly not the type to grovel.

He called again.

And again.

And again.

Every day. I'd once told him, 'My mother says it's rude to phone before nine in the morning or after nine at night.'

He called at nine and every hour until nine. Never before nine and never after – thirteen times a day – for a whole week. He was relentless. I started to feel sorry for John Frank and understood why he'd dodged his answer machine over those two months.

I changed my answer machine message to: '. . . and if that's Colin, I resign.'

THE POSTMAN ALWAYS RINGS TWICE

As I refused to answer the phone, Colin tried the personal touch. He came to the house – and leant on the front-door buzzer – for days. I was still furious and decided to be as stubborn as he was. I ignored it. And then I worried he might get violent. I feared he was going to get a gun. He'd once told me how easy it is to get hold of one. I tried to calm myself. What was he going to do with a gun anyway? He couldn't get to me. It was easy for me to hide on the second floor. I just kept the curtains closed, kept my head down and the TV turned up. But it didn't disguise the endless buzzing. Colin was subjecting me to my own private screening of *The Swarm*. It droned on for days. It was a siege. I was running out of loo paper. I even thought about calling the police until I realised that might make matters even worse. And then one day it stopped. I didn't find out why until that night.

Colin never gives up. He didn't interpret being alone as a sign that the project was dead. In fact, his resolve was strengthened. He knew there was an audience for his story because of the reactions he'd got from the thousands of people who'd sat in the back of his taxi. He was sure he was right, and he was going to prove it.

It was then that he remembered he couldn't do it on his own. That moment of humility caused a lull in his storm and as the clouds lifted a canny idea floated in on a calm breeze. If he was going to get his message to a lot of people, he needed a lot of messengers. One cab driver foghorning around Soho would never be enough. He needed the loudest loudhailer there is: he needed the press.

He went to Fleet Street. Not the actual Fleet Street because the press don't work there any more. Instead, he went to Canary Wharf, where he was hailed by Catherine Milner. Catherine was the Arts Correspondent for the *Sunday Telegraph*. It was late on a Saturday afternoon and she wanted to be dropped at Bank, the nearest Tube station to

Canary Wharf. She chose a cab to get her to the Tube because she didn't want to use the light railway link; it's empty at the weekend and she didn't feel safe on her own. On the way to Bank, Colin told her his property scam had gone horribly wrong and that he'd been left penniless. He told her a mystery Hollywood hotshot had inspired him to get his story written down. When they reached Bank, Catherine's notebook was already filling and, as she wanted to hear the rest of the story, they continued their journey to Notting Hill Gate.

Colin told her how he'd found the writer, director and cast from his taxi. And that his executive producer was the man who'd won an Oscar for *Taxi Driver*. And he'd done *The Sting*. And *Close Encounters of the Third Kind*.

'Wow!' Catherine said. 'That is quite a story.'

'And you've just paid twenty quid to hear it.'

Colin told me all this in person. He'd managed to trick his way into my building by waiting outside the front door until one of my neighbours arrived. He then tail-coated his way in and knocked on my front door. I was surprised to see him. I was surprised because he was grinning from ear to ear.

He didn't start by offering the apology I

thought I deserved. 'You'd better change your message,' he said first.

'What part of "I resign" don't you understand, Colin?'

'You're about to get a call from the *Sunday Telegraph*. They want to know how you feel about making a movie in Hollywood.'

I was getting nervous. I started to feel damp – everywhere.

'What are you talking about?'

'I told them we're about to sign a huge deal.' He was still grinning.

'Have CineCentury changed their minds about Tim Roth?' I asked, guessing the answer.

'No, but the *Telegraph* don't know that.' I couldn't believe it. His grin was getting wider.

'I don't want to talk to the press, Colin. What do you expect me to say?' I could hear the panic in my voice.

'Whatever it takes,' Colin said.

'I'm not going to lie,' I said at too high a pitch.

'Why not?'

'My father reads the *Telegraph*.'

CITIZEN KANE

I didn't expect a journalist to be charming. Catherine Milner was. When she phoned, it didn't feel like an inquisition at all.

'I've just heard Colin's amazing story.' I could hear her smiling. He'd done a good job on her.

'It is something of a story,' I said cautiously, hoping she wouldn't see through my sarcasm.

'What do you think you'll earn?'

It was going to be worse than I'd feared.

'I can't talk figures at this stage.' I still hadn't lied.

'When does the film go into production?'

I think I started to twitch.

'Oh, I'm only the writer. That's out of my hands.' I knew I was coming across as the guy who'd missed all the meetings, but that was better than lying.

'Well, I'd love to ask you more, but if I'm going to get this filed for tomorrow, I'd better get busy,' she said and hung up. I hadn't lied.

I phoned Colin.

'How'd it go?'

'I didn't lie.'

'So, are we partners again?' he said.

'I suppose so. But if you ever make a decision again without speaking to me first . . .'

'What? About things like speaking to the press?' he said, goading cheekily.

But I wasn't angry. He'd stopped at nothing to get me back.

AROUND THE WORLD
IN EIGHTY DAYS

In the very small hours of Sunday, 27 April 1997, I was too excited to sleep. I was wondering whether Catherine's story was going to appear. Surely she'd realise we were just a couple of idiots having a go.

It was approaching dawn when I remembered there was a stand outside King's Cross Station that sold Sunday papers early. By the time I got there, the sky was ajar and the sun had just started to bleach the clouds. I rushed to the stand but the *Sunday Telegraph* delivery had yet to arrive. I leant against some railings and found myself staring at an elongated reflection in the mirrored front of a burger joint. It was me – and I looked awful. I had bags under my eyes that would have been the envy of Phileas Fogg. I moved away from my exhausted doppelganger and, wanting to hide, put on some sunglasses. While I scanned every delivery van, I avoided eye contact with the tragic cast of raggedy winos who were refusing to leave the stage even though last night's curtain had come down some time before.

Suddenly a smelly drunk was a foot away, staring up at me. I turned away, hoping he'd do the same, but he'd locked on and was following my double-glazed gaze. I would have looked a ridiculous poseur wearing sunglasses at five-thirty in the morning.

'Is your future so bright you have to wear shades?' he belched. I said nothing. Colin would have known how to reply.

Then I saw a man with a *Sunday Telegraph* under his arm. The papers had arrived while I was being entertained by the dypso. I ran to the stand and grabbed a copy. There were several sections to the paper and at first I couldn't find the Arts one. Then I found it hidden behind the children's cartoon section. But our story wasn't there. The editor must have hated the story. Or Catherine must have changed her mind. Or maybe she was going to wait till the film was out. Either way, she must have seen through me and realised there was no deal.

I went home deflated. While the kettle boiled, I flicked through the main news section. When I got to page four, I saw it. It was huge. The article covered the top half of the page. There were hundreds of words. There was a large picture of Colin. And some smaller ones of Graham Baker, Tim Roth, Neil Jordan and, for some reason, Colin Firth. And the headline: CABBIE HITS THE ROAD TO HOLLYWOOD. And a sub: Story told in London taxi set to be $15M movie. What the hell had Colin told her?

THE 39 STEPS

As soon as I'd read Catherine's article, I phoned Colin, but he got in the first word.

'Have you seen the *Sunday Mirror*?' He was delighted with himself. 'Page two. It says we're sharing five point nine million.' Colin chuckled.

'Where'd they get that from?'

'Not me,' Colin said. 'I've got to go. That's my phone. I've got another editor on line three!'

And the phone didn't stop ringing all day. I didn't realise the papers stole each other's stories. It's obvious when you think about it. How else would the wildfire spread? But I didn't realise it was so flagrant. Every other paper wanted the lottery-winning story of the lowly cab driver who'd made it in Hollywood. They called Colin first. Then he called me to warn of their imminent call. Then, one minute later, they'd call to confirm the lowly cab driver wasn't lying. Frankly, it didn't matter what I said. After a while, they stopped calling and simply based their articles on each other's. It's true they make up most of it. Being quoted by people you've never met is an odd way to spread the word.

I couldn't believe how fast the papers worked. A swarm of press photographers descended on both of us, and our ugly mugs started appearing in later editions. They got Colin to park his taxi in front of the Odeon in Leicester Square. They wanted to photograph Colin leaping around like a man who'd just won the Lottery, but thankfully he refused. He sat in the front of the cab, loving every minute. I sat in the back and tried to look invisible. It was embarrassing. A small crowd was gathering and people were asking, 'Who the hell are they?' I was too ashamed to answer.

And it wasn't just the press who called. My father phoned to say he'd seen the article in the *Sunday Telegraph*.

'So, you've signed a deal, have you?'

'No, this is all part of an elaborate marketing strategy,' was the best I could come up with without lying.

My mother was delighted by the surprise of it

all and gave me some good advice: 'Try not to scowl in front of the cameras, darling.'

I wanted them to be proud of what we'd done, but I knew I didn't deserve it: I was a fake. But they didn't give me a hard time; telling me off wouldn't silence the press.

Monday was even busier. The TV stations picked up the story and wanted to interview us live. I felt moist about that. I hated the fuss. I tried to get out of it, but ITV wanted to lead with me on the lunchtime news. I suggested Colin would be better, but they needed both of us. They wanted to film him in his taxi while I did the studio interview.

Colin dropped me at Television Centre on the South Bank with ten minutes to spare. I waited in reception looking out for celebrities, but the only person I saw was the guy who played the editor in *Drop the Dead Donkey*, the TV comedy about the press. A delightful young assistant busied over to collect me and treated me like I was a superstar. I was uncomfortable with all the grovelling. I was even more uncomfortable when people started talking about make-up.

I said no thank you, but refusing it wasn't an option. My albino visage positively screamed out for airbrushing. They call it slap for a good reason. By the time the smiley-smiley make-up girl was done, I had so much fake tan on I looked like I'd fallen into a vat of creosote.

The news music started and the delightful assistant dashed into the make-up room to get me. In the backstage gloom, I did well to avoid tripping over all the cables and stands that surrounded the set. Mary Nightingale was going to present the news that day. She sat elegantly in the hot seat, coolly shuffling her script. I always thought those papers were a prop and that the whole thing was done on autocue, but she seemed to be learning her lines. The set design put her desk in front of a huge window. She was framed by a view of the Thames and London beyond. I fell into the guest chair next to Mary and she flashed me a welcoming smile. There's a bizarre intimacy about meeting for the first time a woman you watch every night.

A hurried soundman struggled to clip a microphone to the particularly thick lapel of my jacket. They don't like to use your shirt in case they pick up an anxious heart pinballing around your rib cage. And then my demure interrogator was introducing our story.

'A London cab driver has just sold his story to a Hollywood producer he met in the back of his taxi. The taxi driver is Colin Hayday and he's in Leicester Square with Eamonn Holmes . . .'

Across the set was a monitor and I watched it cut from Mary to Eamonn. Colin did his bit. He was relaxed and cocky, but he was also charming, and he and Eamonn seemed to get on. Colin was hilarious, but I couldn't enjoy it because every second that went by drew me ever closer to lying on national television. Mary was obviously going to ask me how I felt about selling a film we hadn't actually sold. And I was absolutely not going to lie. And my father might be watching. And then I saw my face on the monitor. And, bloody hell, I was a funny colour. And I was scowling. I forget what I said, but I imagine I came across as extremely odd. More than that, I was unhelpful. She was asking all the obvious questions, expecting me to be delighted by our success, and instead I was squirming like Mr Bean. I mumbled about anything – the weather, public transport – anything that allowed me to avoid her questions. I probably sounded like a politician.

I couldn't wait to get back to the make-up room to get off my slap. While I scrubbed my face clean, I overheard the old boy sitting in the make-up chair next to me. He was a judge and was asking whether he could keep the make-up on after he'd done his interview. There are some oddballs out there. And some of them are on national television.

A MAN FOR ALL SEASONS

I detested the whole press fuss. Colin loved it. I must say, he was sensational. While I refused to do another interview, Colin tiptoed between the cameras like a lion tamer. He dodged awkward questions by extolling the benefits of networking. He insisted that meeting people was the only way to change your life and would turn for a close-up and tell the world: 'Stop waiting for life to come to you.' Or: 'Get out there. Meet people. Ask them the most interesting thing that's ever happened to them.'

I couldn't bear the thought of lying, whereas Colin effortlessly deflected any probing query with anecdotes about his millionaire past, or he'd name-drop his famous passengers and confess the audacious things he'd said to them.

One interview Colin particularly loved was with Richard Madeley on *This Morning*. Judy Finnigan was away on the day Colin was a guest; her chair was taken by the late Caron Keating, Gloria Hunniford's daughter. Caron was on particularly sparkling form. She said Colin's life reminded her, by coincidence, of one of my favourite high-concept films, *Groundhog Day*. She pointed out that, just like Bill Murray in the film, Colin woke up every day and had to put the pieces of his package together again.

Richard, not surprisingly for a seasoned chat-show host, is well connected and knew all the people Colin referred to. Richard's style is to indulge his guests; he encouraged Colin's audacity and as Colin's pitch became relentless he played along. He put his feet up on the coffee table, revealing the well-stitched soles of a smart pair of Chelsea boots, and graciously let Colin take over the show. When the show was over, most of the crew gave Colin their business cards and offered to work on the film.

The most ridiculous trick in that day's media circus became our slot on *News at Ten*. Of all the interviews Colin had done that day, we didn't know one of them was going to be the 'And finally . . .' section that Trevor McDonald himself was going to introduce. Because we were such amateurs, we did the TV interviews in the order Colin's mobile rang. We ran a strictly first-come, first-served system. It seemed the fairest method. A proper PR person will tell you there is a vitally important pecking order that should be respected at all times. As we didn't know this, we kept ITN waiting – for hours. ITN are PR royalty and we kept their camera crew, recently returned from Bosnia, waiting in the street while Colin was interviewed by a sweet girl from channel nothing. In the PR hierarchy, she was below the first rung. She even operated the camera herself on a tripod in Charlotte Street. ITN would have to wait. We had agreed to her first and refused to bump her. My father always taught me there's never any reason to be rude. Who did ITN think they were anyway? I think they were more offended when Colin said, 'Who do I see about getting paid?'

'What do you mean?' the ITN sound guy said.

'You're getting paid, aren't you? If you're getting paid, I'm getting paid.'

And he meant it. He refused to do the interview until the whole crew had emptied their pockets of change. Colin forced them to rustle up the princely sum of £34.70 before he'd let them film him.

Colin had a strict rule about the money: he charged everyone. And it was more than just shrapnel: some fifties, some hundreds, some two hundreds, some five hundreds, even some thousands from the tabloids. And it all added up. Most film projects struggle to raise any money at all to cover the 'development' stage of the project, the stage when the script is written. Our project was the only film in history to get its development budget paid for by the press. Colin raised every penny, but he split it with me fifty-fifty.

CASINO ROYALE

By the end of that week, the press interest was bordering on harassment. That's the way I saw it. But Colin still loved it. While he stayed in London to deal with the other formats, such as the radio, I abandoned my phone and fled to my sister's house in the country. As all the fuss had made me conscious of the wide audience my script might encounter, pride made me polish it once more. And I couldn't buff with the phone ringing all day.

While I was enjoying the stillness of normality, the incredible story of Colin's antics was journeying around the world – most significantly to the United States. ABC, CBS, NBC and apparently every other TV channel that traded by three initials picked up his dream-come-true story and took it in turns to lead the cheer. I was devastated. It was bad enough lying to the country. We were now lying to the world.

Then CineCentury heard about it. We were unaware of this crucial fact until Sarah phoned Colin. While she'd been fielding calls from all the actors' agents who'd heard the fuss about the film she was casting, her fax machine whirred into life. She saw CineCentury's letterhead first, upside down. Then the zeros. All twelve of them. Colin's antics had convinced them the world was ready for the story of a cab-driving con man. They would pay five million dollars for an actor to play Colin and the same for an actor to play the lawyer.

'WE'VE DONE IT!' Colin screamed.

When he told me the numbers, I stayed silent. There was nothing else to say; he'd got the money.

Lightning had struck.

CABARET

Celebration should be encouraged at every opportunity. Not just for the big stuff but for every step along the way. It's all too easy to put off enjoying each hint of success because your eye has moved on to the next hurdle.

We soon found out there was some small print attached to CineCentury's offer, but nothing to take the shine off our victory. They were indeed prepared to pay ten million for the leads, but they still had final approval and, annoyingly, they still didn't think Tim Roth was right for the part. But as we had millions of dollars to find the right man, we decided it was time to drink something fizzy. Colin chose a suitably optimistic venue. We met in the Windows On The World Bar on the lofty penthouse floor of the Park Lane Hilton.

The bar has a spectacular view across Hyde Park and west London. It was early evening when we arrived. I ordered a vodka and tonic because I thought the place felt very James Bond. Colin ordered a Coke because he always does.

'So who *are* we going to get to play Colin?' I asked.

'Whoever it takes,' Colin said.

'Maybe we should change our minds and cast Colin as your age,' I said. 'That'll open things up a bit.'

'We'll think of someone,' Colin said.

I looked out over a bustling West End and laughed at our situation.

'What?' he said.

'I was just admiring the irony. You did all of this for the money. Now you've got millions and nothing to spend it on.'

'I didn't just do it for the money,' Colin said quietly.

I was going to ask him to explain, but we were interrupted by the waiter, who made a meal of serving the olives and the mixed nuts and the folded napkins and the placemats and finally our drinks. When he'd gone, we raised our glasses to make a toast. Colin beat me to it.

'To status,' he said. I was expecting something less profound – and less serious.

'Let me tell you something.' And he told me about another time he'd fallen on hard times; when he'd lost the money from the clubs that he'd put into property and had been forced to go back to driving the taxi. A peacock of a man had got in looking pleased with himself. The man had just bought a new watch and was admiring it. Colin recognised the brand from the distinctive octagonal shape of its bezel. Before their conversation had even started, Colin said, 'Audemars Piguet. Royal Oak series.' The man was impressed. Audemars Piguet is a rare Swiss make. He was pleased Colin had acknowledged his ten-grand watch until he saw the same watch on Colin's wrist – in gold. Colin's cost double. He hadn't sold it because it was the last thing he had to remind him of the good times.

'Is that real?' the peacock had asked.

'Of course.'

'How can you afford that? I'm the managing director of British Steel and I can only afford the steel one.'

I was a little confused. 'So you *did* do it for the money?'

'*No*. Self-respect. When you've had it and lost it, you want it back.'

Colin threw back a peanut.

I noticed he was wearing a cheap Casio.

'So you won't be upgrading your watch, then?'

Colin didn't laugh. He was suddenly looking uncomfortable.

'Are you all right?'

He was pressing his forearm across his abdomen.

'I've got a dreadful tummy ache,' he whispered. Tummy wasn't a word I expected Colin to use.

'Try standing. Sitting down might be crunching you up.' As I said it, I realised how amateurish a medic I sounded. Colin stood with some difficulty and shuffled to the lift. I went after him but not before dropping a twenty-pound note on our table. I remember hoping I looked very James Bond by paying without waiting for the bill.

On the way down in the lift, Colin was swaying backwards and forwards like a man who'd just been gut-punched in a gold-rush brawl.

'Do you think it was the nuts?'

He didn't answer. I was starting to think it might be serious. As soon as the lift got to the lobby, he rushed outside and hobbled round the corner to where his cab was parked and doubled up to be sick in the gutter by the rear wheel. I took a clean handkerchief from my top pocket. As Colin had his back to me, I passed the handkerchief over his shoulder. He wiped his mouth. Then he was sick again, more painfully.

A couple of French students walked by with their noses in guidebooks. They looked up to see Colin being sick and both tutted loudly before saying to each other in scolding tones, '*Les anglais.*'

'*Et il est un chauffeur.*'

I was amazed Colin didn't answer back.

WATERSHIP DOWN

The hurtling ambulance bee-barred Colin to the nearest Accident & Emergency department. They scanned him and poked him and prodded him and rushed him away for surgery. I only found out what was wrong when I visited his room at Roding Hospital, a private practice in Redbridge, Essex. I was impressed he'd managed to go private. Perhaps unfairly, I wondered whether he was scamming again, but he wasn't; he was more cautious than I'd realised and had kept up his medical insurance.

At reception, I followed the direction of the nurse's finger to his room and was surprised to see a small crowd of smartly dressed visitors around his bed.

I stopped outside the door and considered waiting until some of the visitors had gone, but one of them spotted me loitering and stared, prompting the others to peer as well. They were as fearless as Colin. I guessed they were his family.

'Who is it?' I heard Colin say from inside the room. I couldn't see him, but I was bemused to hear he was still in charge despite sounding so weak. I walked in, self-conscious about interrupting the party, and smiled a hello at everyone. Sitting in a chair by Colin's pillow was a beautiful silver-haired lady whom I assumed to be his mother, Hannah. There were two other women: his sisters, Tina and Julie. The other relation was John, Colin's brother. I didn't know Colin had an identical twin. The thought of two of them didn't bear thinking about right then.

Colin was beaming at me like I was some sort of prodigal son. Despite his smile, he looked awful. Sunken eyes. Sunken cheeks. Sunken everything. He was lying on the bed in elegant striped pyjamas and a silk dressing gown. He looked like Noel Coward. I shuffled to his bed and leaned over to offer my hand. He reached up, held my shoulder and pulled me close. We hugged. We'd never hugged before. Colin is not a sentimental man and the affection in the gesture was touching. And frightening. For so chilled a man to melt so completely could mean only one thing. His news must have been bad.

It was worse than bad.

'It's cancer,' he whispered.

That truly appalling word prompted Colin's mother to raise a tissue to her eye. Colin reached a hand across to her.

'Don't cry, Ma.' Colin sounded gentle but firm. 'You don't need to. I'm going to sort this.'

'I'm sorry, darling,' she said, squeezing Colin's hand so hard his knuckles frosted.

'Don't be sorry. Be strong.'

'I will, my darling,' she said in the delicate voice of a mother comforting her five year old. 'Now, you talk to your friend.' She smiled sweetly at me then touched a tender kiss to her son's forehead before leading her three healthy children out of the room. All their heads were bowed. Colin's predicament was so overwhelming, so much the focus of everyone's attention, we visitors had refrained from any conversation other than acknowledging each other with silence. No one was being rude. It was simply that we all read the situation the same: we all knew we would have time to talk later – and Colin might not.

Colin's mother did well to stifle her tears until she got out into the corridor. I know Colin heard her, but he said nothing.

'Didn't you feel anything?' I asked.

'I had dreadful tummy aches, but you don't whinge about that, do you?'

I asked him about his operation and whether the staff were looking after him. But there was one question I avoided. I was wondering whether the constant strain of keeping our film alive had ignited his cancer.

TO KILL A MOCKINGBIRD

The surgeon had to remove eighty per cent of Colin's stomach. But there was worse to come. In the form of one word, no less ugly for being abbreviated, chemo.

Chemotherapy is the real C-word in the world of cancer. The idea of cancer is terrifying for many obvious reasons, but one real horror is the thought of having to undergo chemotherapy. It seems a drastic remedy. There's no avoiding that chemotherapy kills you to cure you. Colin's assessment was less melodramatic. His approach was as practical as ever. If chemo worked, and the experts told him it did, then he would do whatever had to be done to get better.

'Whatever it takes,' he said.

Colin's treatment was administered intravenously. Two months after the operation, to give him time to recover from his surgery, a nurse put a cannula in the top of his right hand. This was connected to a tube that led to a transparent one-litre bag that hung from a stand over his head. Inside the bag, the chemotherapy agent had been pre-mixed with clear saline and looked innocent enough. But the nurse was handling the bag with thick rubber gloves. If it leaked and she got any of the fluid on her skin, the agent would cause burns. And that same fluid was going into Colin's veins. It doesn't burn because in the vein there's nothing to fan the flames. In fact, it feels cold because the bag is stored in a fridge. Colin said it was comfortable enough, if a little creepy. I recount all this not to frighten anybody who might have to face chemotherapy but to forewarn them about what to expect. Chemotherapy is frightening but less frightening than the fear of the unknown.

Colin had six sessions in total, each one three to four weeks apart. The sessions have to be spaced apart to give the body time to recover from the onslaught. There are dozens of chemotherapy drugs and they all work in clever ways to kill cancer cells and inhibit their spread to other parts.

of the body. For example, some agents neuter the chromosomes and stop the cells from forming in the first place. Some kill the cell from the outside by weakening the cell wall. It's ingenious stuff, but it also sparks an internal battle that sometimes brings with it an infamous side effect: hair loss. This isn't always the case, but it happened to Colin.

Sometimes an ice cap, similar to a swimmer's cap but frozen, worn during the treatment can prevent hair loss. By chilling the scalp, the blood vessels serving the hair follicles become less active and less likely to take up the toxic chemicals. Colin didn't buy this theory. It was probably too fussy for him. Or maybe he felt it wasn't macho. Again, practicality paved his path, and he thought he'd beat the chemo to it. After his first session, he went straight to the barber and had his head shaved.

One side effect everyone undergoing chemotherapy seems to suffer is extreme exhaustion. Colin was no different. Every time I called him, I was sure I'd woken him up, but he always laughed it off and asked after me. I wished I had good news about the film to cheer him up, but the project seemed to go into turnaround without him at the helm.

Soon after the operation, I'd told John Frank the

awful news. Even though he and Colin had not always got on, John Frank was genuinely devastated and insisted we let Colin concentrate on recovery. He meant well and was probably trying to remind me that Colin's health was the priority. But as I knew Colin would hate his cancer to be used as an excuse to drop the project, I phoned John Frank again with a few lame casting suggestions for CineCentury. They politely ignored the subject. I understood why. It was a delicate situation. And an ironic one: I knew and they knew that no actor was big enough to play Colin just at the time when he was wasting away. As they wanted to avoid offending Colin by saying that his best hadn't been good enough, they stayed quiet. I like to think Hollywood's silence was meant as a gesture of respect, but they were being pessimistic: they were anticipating Colin's death.

Colin and I avoided talking about the film because the subject reminded us of lost opportunities. But even though we had no leading actor at that point, we hoped a hot new star would appear.

'At the very least,' I told Colin, 'we've got the package for when you're better.'

My claim was tenuous, but he didn't dispute it. He needed a simple dream for the future because his present goal had to be recovery.

THE ENGLISH PATIENT

Everything changed. Aside from the effects of the chemo, the loss of most of Colin's stomach forced him to change his diet radically. His formerly healthy appetite vanished and he became a grazer. A quarter of a sandwich became a banquet. As he had hardly any stomach to hold and digest the food he ate, he had to nibble. This meant he was always running on empty. In fact, he was digesting so little he had to have vitamin B6 injections every month to give him the energy to walk.

Colin's reduced food consumption inevitably led to alarming weight loss. His athletic six foot one and a half-inch frame shed sixty pounds in a month. When I visited him, the exhausted creature who let me in, always in his dressing gown, had become so thin and blue from the cold he looked like a human light sabre – only without the glow. If Colin had even been half the man he was before, he would have been pleased. In fact, exhaustion became such an issue for him, he rented a ground-floor flat because he couldn't go up stairs. Things were not looking up.

BLADE RUNNER

Colin had never been a patient man until he became a patient. As he'd spent every waking minute developing a Hollywood movie, doing nothing every day was frustrating. And then he realised he was marking off the milestones on his journey to total recovery. Every day when nothing happened was a day when the tumour wasn't happening.

Six months after his operation, the phone rang in Colin's viewless flat.

'Is that Colin?' The accent was American.

'Who's that?' Colin asked, intrigued.

'This is Michael.' Colin was amazed. They'd never spoken before. Michael Phillips had heard about Colin's cancer from John Frank. He also knew we'd failed to come up with a bankable star for CineCentury.

Michael's call gave an optimist like Colin the hope that the project was about to be rekindled. He hoped Michael wanted to get hands-on at last. He hoped his cancer might have prompted Michael to do him the ultimate favour and finish the job Colin had started. But Michael was phoning because he'd heard just how ill Colin was. He didn't mention the film. Maybe it was embarrassing for him because he knew that, in effect, Colin had fired him when he'd fired John Frank.

Finally, Colin couldn't resist: 'I couldn't keep all the balls in the air.'

'It's the same for every producer,' Michael said. Colin liked being called a producer by an Oscar winner.

'Worst of all, Michael, I got the money, but I couldn't find anyone to play me.' Colin laughed.

Michael summed it up with the wisdom that won him an Oscar.

'The lightning went away.'

Even though Michael's phone call confirmed the total collapse of the project, Colin refused to dwell on the loss. He was happy to be alive. This is perhaps no surprise. When someone is hanging on to what might be the last days of life itself, a two-hour film is not very important.

ENCHANTED APRIL

I remember when I first thought Colin might recover. It was more than a year after his operation. I went to his flat, and he surprised me by greeting me in new jeans, an ironed white shirt and a Yankees baseball cap, a present from his nephew, Danny, in the States. Colin was still bald and emaciated, but he'd become extremely sprightly.

'Come in,' he said. 'Hope you don't mind – got the taxman coming round – wouldn't take no for an answer.' I was worried he was putting on a show of being fitter than he was.

'Don't tire yourself,' I said, but he waved away my pampering concern.

'Help yourself to a cup of tea,' he said, striding across to his bedroom. 'I've got to get changed.' I didn't understand this because he was already smart enough.

'Can I get you one?' I asked.

'Coffee, please.'

That surprised me. In all the time I'd known Colin, he'd only ever drunk tea, and lots of it, unless he was drinking Coke. He told me he thought his treatments had altered his taste buds. He still liked Coke, but now he hated the taste of tea. I smiled at the irony as he shouted the explanation from the bedroom.

'At least I won't have to hear that bloody two sugars stirred once to the left bollocks again,' I said, teasingly. 'How do you want your coffee?' I shouted from the kitchen.

'One sugar, please. Stirred twice to the right,' he said, laughing before he'd got to the end of his sentence.

Colin reappeared wearing a market-stall tracksuit.

'I don't think you're quite ready for the gym,' I said.

'I need to look poor,' Colin said, taking off his baseball cap. The baldness still shocked me. Colin noticed my reaction.

'Bit weird, isn't it?' Colin suggested, rubbing his pate. 'I've lost it everywhere, you know.' I didn't want to dwell on the extent of Colin's hairlessness, but he continued. 'The other day I looked down at my three-piece suite. My bloody pubes are gone. Bald as a coot, I am. Look like the last turkey in the shop.' I had to laugh. He was clearly coping.

'Anyway, how do I look?' he asked again.

It seemed unfair to answer truthfully. 'OK,' I lied.

'Damn,' he moaned. 'How about this?' He slumped his shoulders and pulled the hangdog face of an old witch. I understood his game: he wanted to look as ill as possible for the taxman.

'Awful,' I said.

'Good.' He laughed.

Then the doorbell went.

'Can you get that? I'm too ill,' he said, reclining on the sofa.

I buried my mirth and grimly led the taxman into the sitting room. The taxman was as wide as he was tall. He had the dimensions of a tick box, which was appropriate as he already had his clipboard out of his briefcase. Colin made an exaggerated fuss of trying to struggle to his feet to greet his guest.

'Please stay seated,' the taxman urged him.

'Thank you, mate,' Colin said, panting heavily for effect. 'It's so good of you to come round,' Colin added. 'Can I make you a cup of tea, *mate*?'

Colin was treating him like his new best friend.

The taxman shook his head. 'I won't trouble you long.'

'How can I help?' Colin wheezed. And coughed.

'Our records show an unpaid return from '96. A little over two thousand pounds.'

Colin rubbed his bald head for effect. 'You're kidding,' he moaned.

The taxman shook his head firmly.

'Look, mate,' Colin said. 'I'll be honest with you.' That was a good line. 'I've got cancer and I haven't worked for a bloody long time. I've got a long list of debts and you're a long way from the bottom.'

'Don't you mean the top?' said the taxman, confused.

'No,' stressed Colin. 'You're definitely not near the top. And you're not near the bottom – because I'm afraid you ain't even on the list.'

Awkward silence.

Colin wrapped his bony fingers round his bony knees and pulled himself forward. He held himself bowed forward as if in a confessional box.

'I'm really sorry, mate. What do you want me to say?'

The taxman said nothing, but his expression became compassionate.

'So you haven't got any savings?' the taxman said. The tone of his voice implied he was telling Colin what to say.

'That's right,' Colin said sorrowfully. The taxman ticked a box on his form.

'And you haven't got any sickness insurance?' He was definitely leading the witness.

'You're right again, mate.' The taxman checked another box. Then he handed the clipboard to Colin.

'Could you sign there, please?'

Colin did his laboured signature and handed back the clipboard. The taxman stood up.

'Thank you, Mr Hayday. I'll see myself out.'

'Is that it?' Colin said chirpily, forgetting to wheeze.

'Sometimes we have to make a commercial decision. Some debts simply aren't worth chasing,' the taxman said. I was stunned by his generosity.

'They're wrong, aren't they?' Colin said, back to his cryptic games.

'I'm sorry?' said the taxman, perplexed.

'You're not all wankers, are you?' Colin beamed wistfully.

The taxman smiled. We were at rock bottom, but Colin's luck was changing. Or as he would put it: he was changing his luck.

THE MERCHANT
OF VENICE

At last, five years later, Colin got the all-clear from his consultant, the surgeon he'd renamed 'The Professor' out of respect and gratitude for saving his life.

Colin hadn't done much in the time it had taken him to recover, but he'd come to terms with his new life. He'd got himself a disabled badge for his cab to prove he had no hang-ups about his incapacity. He even saw the upside of having the badge: it gave him his dream of being able to park wherever he wanted.

He used all his free time to catch up with his large family and see all the films I'd been insisting he watch over the years. His VCR became his personal reference library and his sofa his new favourite driving seat. His dyslexia veiled most of the subtlety of my subtitled favourites: *The Wages of Fear*, *The Rules of the Game* and *The Bicycle Thief*. But we agreed wholeheartedly we wouldn't mind shaking hands with Cool Hand Luke, Dirty Harry and any character played by Peter Sellers.

Colin's newly encyclopedic knowledge of world cinema meant he was particularly looking forward to watching the 2002 edition of the Oscars ceremony on TV. He was halfway through what was to be a record-breaking four-hour-and-sixteen-minute show when yet another sweeping shot of the auditorium cut to a close-up of yet another special guest. This one had a beard. Colin moved closer to the set. The special guest had glasses.

'I don't fucking believe it,' Colin said out loud.

Was it him? Surely not. Could it possibly be? And then Whoopi Goldberg introduced 'Mister Francis Ford Coppola'. Colin's mentor – Mr-If-You're-Good-Enough-You'll-Find-Me – had been the Godfather himself.

My phone rang at two in the morning. I'd only just given up on the live Oscars myself and gone to bed. I was still awake and I answered quickly because the phone was in the bedroom and my girlfriend was asleep. It was useless me trying to be quiet because Colin's scream woke her up. And she was glad he did because what he shouted was: 'I FOUND THE BEARD!'

It had taken him ten years: Colin had been good enough.

EMPIRE OF THE SUN

The next day, Colin phoned Coppola's office in California.

'Can I speak to Francis?'

'Can I say who's calling?' The receptionist was suspicious of this new accent being so familiar.

'Colin Hayday. He knows me. He heard my story in my taxi in London ten years ago.'

Of course his outrageous claim wasn't believed. The receptionist refused to lose her job by failing to vet this limey clown. Instead, she transferred Colin to the Acquisitions Department, but probably not before warning them the caller was a crank from Great Britain. Bobby Rock, head of acquisitions, continued the call. Colin told Bobby he'd met his boss and been invited to send in a script.

'Well, send me the script,' said Bobby dryly. Colin sensed Bobby also didn't believe him. He was worried the script was destined to be shredded and dropped into the receptionist's trash can.

'I tell you what,' Colin said. 'I'll do better than that. I'll deliver it myself.'

Colin called me after that. 'I'm off to Hollywood. It's time to get some plates spinning.'

'Are you safe to travel?'

'I've checked with the Professor and he says I'm fine.'

Colin's mother was nervous about him travelling alone. I couldn't go because a writing job had come along and I needed it badly. Frankly, I was skint. If you linked all the minus signs on my bank statements together, they would have reached Los Angeles, but that was as close as I could afford to get to Hollywood.

Colin went with his twin brother, John. There was something appropriate about the before and after of this travelling pair. Colin, still four stone lighter than before, would point to his brother and say, 'This is what I used to look like before the cancer. Only I was better looking.'

John used to retort, 'Colin's the only man I know who has to run round the shower to get wet.' Colin always laughed at that one. Being prepared to joke about his situation made him easy company. It wasn't his style to play the victim.

It was this winner's spirit that prompted Colin to stay in the Beverly Hills Hotel. If they were going to do Hollywood, they were going to do it properly. John carried the bags. Colin carried the script. The first thing Colin did when they arrived in LA was call Bobby Rock to say he was in town. Bobby didn't say much, but he did say, 'Leave the script at reception.' Colin was put out by this because Bobby still sounded disinterested. Colin kept his manners and didn't make a fuss, but he told his brother John as soon as he put the phone down, 'We come the best part of four thousand bloody miles and he won't even see us. It's not even him I want to see.'

'Let's get a drink,' said John. It's his favourite line apparently.

They sat at the bar and started a game of star-spotting before their ice-laden drinks had even arrived. Colin had a Coke and John had something stronger. John spotted Diane Keaton, but no other stars were in the ascendant that evening. Eventually, one nil down, Colin got up to go to the loo. While he was away, a man sat down on the bar stool two away from John. When Colin returned, he sat where he'd been sitting before, which meant he was sitting between his brother and the stranger. As it would have been rude for Colin to ignore the man at his elbow, he struck up a conversation. The man was an author called Norman Bogner. I confess I didn't know who Norman Bogner was, but I was in the minority because Norman is a popular man. He's sold well over twenty million books. Colin was impressed by that many zeros and told Norman, 'Even if you only got a buck a book, you must be one rich man.'

Norman was intrigued by Colin's unique combination of front and flattery. They started off talking about London, where Norman had worked for some time, and then Colin told him why he was in LA. When he was finished, Norman said, 'You should speak to my wife, Bettye. She's an agent.'

The next morning, the phone rang in the twins' twin room. Colin answered.

'Norman's been raving about your story,' said Bettye McCartt. 'I understand you're not here long. Can you come to my office today?'

Two hours later, Colin and John were shown in to Bettye's smart office at TAA, The Artists' Agency, one of the biggest agencies in LA. Bettye was delightful and introduced Colin to a tall man who was just leaving.

'This is my friend Michael.'

As Colin likes to tell his story to as large an audience as possible, he launched in before Michael could leave the room. Colin took a deep breath and told them how he met an upper-class lawyer and they'd bought a skyscraper with no money and swapped it for fifty million in diamonds but it had gone dangerously wrong and then he met Coppola who said get a script but he couldn't because he was dyslexic but then he picked up a screenwriter and then Michael Phillips and then the director Graham Baker and then the writer quit but he got him back by using the press to prove they had a good story and they went mad for it so a distributor came up with ten million to pay for the actors and then he got cancer and he couldn't keep all the plates spinning so the whole thing sort of melted away.

'But I'm back,' concluded Colin forcefully. 'I'm over here – I'm not going to say the English are coming, but I am going to get this script to Coppola.' And he dropped the script neatly onto Bettye's desk.

It was one hell of a pitch. Everyone was speechless. Except Michael. He leant forward and tapped the script twice.

'That's not the story,' he said.

'What do you mean?' Colin asked, perplexed. He thought he'd done well.

'Sure, everyone loves a good scam, but that's not the story. The story is the cab driver who takes on Hollywood and produces a film from his cab. He's the guy who just won't give up.'

Then he smiled and left the room.

'Who was he?' Colin asked Bettye.

'That was Michael Eisner,' Bettye said, smiling.

'Who the hell's Michael Eisner?' John said.

'The head of Disney,' Colin said. 'Watch your mouth.'

MISERY

Yet again my phone rang at two in the morning.

'Colin,' I moaned. 'This had better be an emergency.'

'It is an emergency,' he shouted.

I panicked. 'Are you all right?'

'Yeah, yeah. I've just met Michael Eisner. Do you know who he is?'

'The head of Disney.'

'Know what he said?'

'He didn't suggest Mickey Mouse should drive the cab?'

'No. He said we're flogging the wrong story.' I didn't understand why Colin sounded so pleased.

'What are you talking about?'

'He liked the scam, but what he really liked was the story of the story.'

'What do you mean?' My heart was starting to sink.

'That's what I said to him. He said the story is about a taxi driver who takes Hollywood for a ride. He produces a film from the front seat of his cab.'

'What are you saying, Col? Do I have to revise the script again?' My heart was in free-fall.

'No,' he shouted gleefully. 'We need a whole new script.'

Gravity won. My aorta hit the deck.

'I need to think about this, Col.'

'We'll talk about it tomorrow. I'm coming home.'

A CLOCKWORK ORANGE

The next day, sooner than I'd expected, Colin buzzed my flat. He'd got a cab straight from Heathrow, and I imagine he did most of the talking.

'Good, isn't it?' he said eagerly, as soon as I let him in.

'What? Me having to write another script?'

'But he is right, isn't he?' insisted Colin.

'It's easy for him to say. He doesn't have to throw away seven drafts.'

'But everyone loves the story of the story.'

'Before I write another bloody script, Colin, I've got to be sure the story is right. I can't just blindly follow every idea that's chucked into the ring. To date, people have come up with all sorts of crazy stuff: Colin as a black kid, Colin as the lawyer's bastard brother. The IRA has been suggested. The Mafia. Even the Vatican, for God's sake.'

'Exactly,' agreed Colin, oddly. 'And none of them was right.'

'How do we know the story of the story is right?' I said. 'After all, we don't have a bloody ending. We haven't made the film.'

Colin couldn't answer that one. I felt we were back at the start. No, worse. We'd been climbing the mountain all night and woken up to discover we were just in the foothills; the mountain was still ahead, looming over us.

Then it was my turn to fall into the crevasse.

THE PORTRAIT
OF A LADY

The 13th of July 2003 was without question the worst day of my life. It was the day my darling mother died from cancer. She was too young to die and it all happened too fast. Only one year and one week before, she had discovered that a little lump was in fact two advanced tumours. When she told me the appalling news, I tried desperately to be encouraging. As my only first-hand knowledge of cancer had been Colin's, I initially looked ahead with hope. It turned out to be false. I willed my mother's determined character to generate the same recovery Colin has enjoyed. Colin was my shining example of how people can recover from even the most savage cancer attacks. And indeed my mother's initial reaction to chemotherapy had seemed miraculously positive. She didn't lose her hair or her sense of humour. I remember her hosting a Christmas party only six months before she died; she looked as radiant as a movie star and laughed as heartily as usual, her shoulders dancing up and down as they always did when she laughed. Her guests thought the doctors had misdiagnosed because she was the liveliest person at the party. She certainly didn't look like a lady who was dying.

But the doctors were right. When my mother suddenly got worse, I couldn't believe that the shadow of the Grim Reaper had once again overcast my life. It just wasn't fair. But I shouldn't have been so surprised to encounter cancer so close to home for a second time: cancer is everywhere these days. Just about everyone I know knows somebody who's got it or has had it.

In my mother's last six months, I abandoned the project to look after her with my sister and brother. I still can't go into the inexplicable waste and depthless sadness of that time, but the reason I mention my mother now is because she is responsible for this book.

Mothers are particularly tolerant of their sons. My mother watched me write script after script. She also watched me being rejected. She never saw a script become a film and she knew how much I craved that sense of completion. Being an artist herself, she understood the urge to finish what you've started. It became a chronic issue for her as illness finally stopped her from painting altogether. When she was finally bed-bound, one of her last pleasures was books, even though she didn't have the strength to read them herself. As I sat on her bed, reading to her one glorious June afternoon, she suddenly pointed out that many of my favourite films are based on books. She suggested a tried and tested book might be turned into a film more easily than one of my speculative scripts. I smiled politely, dismissing her advice – I knew she didn't know the intricacies of the film-making process – and carried on reading. But my mother persisted with the notion. She asked my girlfriend, now my beautiful wife, to promise to get me to write a book.

THE SHELTERING SKY

I imagine my reaction to my mother's early death was similar to that of anyone who survives a loved one. I was suddenly desperate to make the most of what's left of life, yet frozen in grief because nothing seems worth doing if it can't be shared with the person who's gone.

I spent many months in a state of manic anxiety, repeatedly making to-do lists that never got crossed out. On every one of those lists was the question of what to do with Michael Eisner's advice to tell the story of the story.

The answer came to me six months after the funeral, while I was hanging one of my mother's paintings in the kitchen. The painting in question is unfinished – hardly started, in fact – but it is significant to me because it was the last canvas my mother worked on. It's large, at four feet wide. The subject is a still life, a line of thirteen different drinking glasses. Some are nearly full, but most are empty. The glasses are arranged as if abandoned on a sideboard after a particularly extravagant party. I found myself staring closely at one of those abandoned glasses. It was the only one close to being completed, but the exquisite detailing in that one glass hinted at how splendid the whole painting would have been. It would have been easy for me to let the symbolism of that abandoned painting spark more sorrow, but I didn't allow that indulgence. I didn't have to. Because, for the first time in months – maybe years – I felt calm. It was then that I decided to finish what I'd started.

I discussed my plan with my wife. She said as wisely as ever, 'Listen to your mother.'

I phoned Colin.
   'How are you?' he said.
   'I've been thinking.'
   'What about?'
   'The story of the story.'
   'What do you want to do?'
   'I think I've found the answer.'
   'You've got the ending?' he said.

'Maybe.'

'Well?' he asked, growing impatient.

'I've been missing the obvious,' I said.

'What do you mean?'

'If you're going to catch lightning in a bottle – you need the bottle.'

'Say again,' he said.

'I'm going to write the book.'

THE END

THE CAST AND CREW

THE TAXI DRIVER/PRODUCER/CON MAN
Colin Hayday (As Himself)

THE LAWYER
Alias Alexander Warwick

THE LAWYER'S BOSS
Alias Edward Smedley

THE DIAMOND BROKER
Alias Margot Di Varga

THE EXECUTIVE PRODUCER
Michael Phillips (As Himself)

THE CO-PRODUCER
John Frank Rosenblum (As Himself)

THE CASTING DIRECTOR
Sarah Crowe (As Herself)

THE DIRECTOR
Graham Baker (As Himself)

THE IRISH DIRECTOR
Neil Jordan (As Himself)

THE DIRECTOR'S AGENT
Jenne Casarotto (As Herself)

THE SEPTEMBER FILMS PRODUCER
Alias Virginia

THE ICM AGENT
Dennis Selinger (As Himself)

THE CO-PRODUCER (FOR CINECENTURY – NAME CHANGED)
Alias Tiffany

THE MUSIC
Robbie Williams, Paul McCartney, Ringo Starr, Björk,
Iron Maiden, Stewart Copeland, Placebo, The Charlatans,
Oasis, William Orbit, Simple Minds (As Themselves)

THE WARDROBE
John Galliano, John Robinson (Jigsaw)
(As Themselves)

THE STAR
Tim Roth (As Himself)

THE STAR'S AGENT
Stephanie Randall (As Herself)

THE AMERICAN AUTHOR
Norman Bogner (As Himself)

THE AMERICAN AGENT
Bettye McCartt (As Herself)

Based On An Idea by Michael Eisner

ACKNOWLEDGEMENTS

Colin and I would like to thank the following for making this book possible:

Sarah Crowe – for sticking by us; John Frank Rosenblum – for suffering us; Michael Phillips and Graham Baker – for saying yes; Tim Roth, Michael Caine, Hugh Grant, Neil Jordan, Bob Hoskins, Robbie Williams, Ringo Starr, Barbara Bach, Paul McCartney, Oasis, Placebo, Björk, John Galliano, John Robinson, Nigel Hawthorne, David Soul, Helen Mirren, Ruby Wax, Michael York, Catherine Zeta Jones, Stewart Copeland, Simple Minds, The Charlatans, Iron Maiden, William Orbit, Colin Firth, Mary Nightingale, Eamonn Holmes, Trevor McDonald, Richard Madeley, Caron Keating and Diane Keaton – for being famous; Stephanie Randall, Jenne Casarotto and Dennis Selinger – for being wise; Catherine Milner – for that first article; Francis Ford Coppola, Norman Bogner, Bettye McCartt and Michael Eisner – for the jump start; Chris Morris – for speaking his mind; Robert Kirby, our genius agent – for his faith; Catherine Vile – for introducing us to him; and the wonderful people at Mainstream – for giving us the bottle.

To our families – we love you.

To our readers – we thank you.

To The Academy . . .